Points of Light

THE ART OF BEING HUMAN

Harold Raley

TotalRecall Publications, Inc.
1103 Middlecreek
Friendswood, TX 77546
281-992-3131 TEL
www.totalrecallpress.com

All rights reserved. Except as permitted under the United States Copyright Act of 1976, No part of this publication may be reproduced, stored in a retrieval system, or transmitted in any form or by any means electronic or mechanical or by photocopying, recording, or otherwise without prior permission of the publisher. Exclusive worldwide content publication / distribution by TotalRecall Publications, Inc.

Copyright © 2017 by: Harold Raley

ISBN: 978-1-59095-536-9
UPC: 6-43977-45366-2

Printed in the United States of America with simultaneous printings in Australia, Canada, and United Kingdom.

FIRST EDITION
1   2   3   4   5   6   7   8   9   10

Judgments as to the suitability of the information herein is the purchaser's responsibility. TotalRecall Publications, Inc. extends no warranties, makes no representations, and assumes no responsibility as to the accuracy or suitability of such information for application to the purchaser's intended purposes or for consequences of its use except as described herein.

The scanning, uploading and distribution of this book via the Internet or via any other means without the permission of the publisher is illegal and punishable by law. Please purchase only authorized electronic editions and do not participate in or encourage electronic piracy of copyrighted materials. Your support of the author's rights is appreciated.

To Vicky

Table of Contents

Article 1: Roads Not Taken 0
Article 2. A Tale of Two Cities 2
Article 3. Pathetic Fallacy 4
Article 4: Inside the University 6
Article 5. A Brief History of Tolerance 8
Article 6. A choice of immortalities? 10
Article 7: A Fish out of Water 12
Article 8: A Forgotten Genius 14
Article 9: A Touch of Religious Sociology 16
Article 10: All Women Were Beautiful 18
Article 11: Old Sayings 20
Article 12: Apocalypse Everywhere 22
Article 13: Baby Talk 24
Article 14: Aliens on a Texas Beach 26
Article 15: View from a Mississippi Window 29
Article 16: Stopped at a Red Light 32
Article 17: Death Row 35
Article 18: Depths and Superficialities 38
Article 19: Going in Circles? 40
Article 20: A Matter of Words 42
Article 21: Cultural Downsizing? 44
Article 22: Love, Marriage, and Some Consequences 46
Article 23: Middle-aged Teens? 48
Article 24: Boredom 50
Article 25: Brotherhood of the Truthful 52
Article 26: Cabeza de Vaca: The Second Saga 54
Article 27: Cervantes and Don Quixote 56
Article 28: Chewing the Fat 58
Article 29: Some Thoughts about Cities 60
Article 30: Chicken Little 62
Article 31: Seasonal Code Words 64
Article 32: Colliding Theories 66
Article 33: Condition or Situation? 68
Article 34: Contagious! 70

Article 35: Dressed for the Occasion 72
Article 36: Drinking in Old Texas 74
Article 37: Early Texas Education 76
Article 38: Preferring the Preferable 78
Article 39: Europe's Inverted Pyramid 80
Article 40: Happiness or Exasperation? 82
Article 41: Facing up to Life 84
Article 42: Familiar Falsehoods 86
Article 43: Forbidden Questions 88
Article 44: Patriot or Traitor? 90
Article 45: Foretelling the Future 92
Article 46: Medicine in Frontier Texas 94
Article 47: Last Picture Show? 96
Article 48: A Post-legal Era? 98
Article 49: Separation of Powers 100
Article 50: Life in the Middle Ages 102
Article 51: A Matter of Time 104
Article 52: The Wild Card of Chance 106
Article 53: To Bathe or not to Bathe 108
Article 54: Voting Old Style 110
Article 55: Life in Three Centuries 112
Article 56: Revolutionary Shortcuts 114
Article 57: More on Revolution 116
Article 58: Inventing the Flat Earth 118
Article 59: The Elephant in the Room 120
Article 60: Neither Here nor There 122
Article 61: Propaganda and Rhetoric 124
Article 62: Women in the Enlightenment 126
Article 63: Varieties of Anti-Americanism 128
Article 64: Meditation on a Mountain Road 130
Article 65: Vacations from Rationality 132
Article 66: Who was Shakespeare? 134
Article 67: Superstition 136
Article 68: Sentimental Geography 138
Article 69: The Westward Urge 140
Article 70: Philosophic Fictions 142
Article 71: Our Preexistent Life 144

Article 72: Our Better Half 146
Article 73: The Age of Ideas 148
Article 74: The Fifth Generation 150
Article 75: Psychic Pollutions 152
Article 76: When Crime Was King 154
Article 77: Ideas and Beliefs 156
Article 78: Machiavellian Ethics 158
Article 79: Roman Replay? 160
Article 80: What Is Philosophy? 162
Article 81: Tyrants and Totalitarians 164
Article 82: A Look at Generations 166
Article 83: Insanity and Other Sayings 168
Article 84: The Sounds of Silence 170
Article 85: Provincialism of the Powerful 172
Article 86: Facial Philosophy 174
Article 87: Noble Obligations 176
Article 88: Speedy Americans 178
Article 89: Sexual or "Sexuate"? 180
Article 90: The Art of Being Human 182
Article 91: The Generosity Principle 184
Article 91: The Disappearing Present 186
Article 92: Propaganda 188
Article 93: Originality 190
Article 94: The Faces of Janus 192
Article 95: The Problem with Critical Thinking 194
Article 96: The Naked Truth 196
Article 97: Miracle Fatigue 198
Article 98: Turning a Deaf Ear or a Blind Eye? 200
Article 99: Questions about Sports 202
Article 100: The End of Poverty, Hunger, and Disease? 204
Article 101: The Insider doctrine 206
Article 102: The Future of Books 208
Article 103: The End of Infinity? 210
Article 104: Unreal Man 212
Article 105: Aaron Burr, Villain or Victim? 214
Article 106: The Origin of Beauty 216
Article 107: Horizons 218

Introduction

Most of the essays in this book first appeared as newspaper columns and differ from the originals only in minor, editorial ways. The real challenge for me, used as I was to academic and fiction writing, was the necessary brevity of the essays. The discipline of having to compress my ideas into a finite word count troubled me at first. Later, however, I was grateful for the experience because it forced me to get to the point and stay strictly on task. Instead of grumbling, I came to relish the challenge and to appreciate journalistic brevity as a special literary form more fitting for our hurried times than the ponderous writings of earlier, more leisurely times.

The themes treated are an entirely different matter. They are far-ranging, and the freedom I surrendered in linguistic spaciousness I gained back in the latitude I had to treat many topics as fairly and clearly as space permitted.

But there is method in what may appear to be unrelated themes. At a near or far remove, and from a variety of perspectives, all rest on the master concepts that undergird all my philosophical work: the uniqueness of human reality, the dignity, humor, and pathos of the person, and the possibilities of life that set it far apart and high above all other earthly realities.

A noted thinker once said that clarity is the courtesy an author extends to the reader. Insofar as my abilities permit, I have tried to add another kindness: word economy, which I understand to mean saying as much as possible in the fewest words. In those cases in which there is neither clarity nor economy, I alone take the blame.

Harold Raley

Article 1:
Roads Not Taken

In high school many of us read some of Robert Frost's poems, including his classic "The Road Not Taken." Its metaphorical power is immense but not forced in a way that would disrupt the simple New England setting. In an age of literary overkill, Frost was the master of artistic understatement. In "Stopping by Woods on a Snowy Evening," to my way of thinking, lyrically and euphonically an even better poem, the poet stops on a snowy road, yielding for a moment to the dark beauties of the deep woods that lure him. To what evil or innocence we cannot know. In any case, the call of duty, repeated for moral emphasis, finally breaks the hypnotic appeal and sends him towards his destination, which can be either plainly literal or endlessly symbolic: /The woods are lovely, dark, and deep, /But I have promises to keep, /And miles to go before I sleep, /And miles to go before I sleep.

Frost was one of our easier assignments. Even as teenagers we had no trouble picking up the road as a metaphor of life. For who among us has not decided to take one road at a crossroads or in life and pondered later what our destiny would have been if we had chosen the one not taken? Or felt in sidelong looks the temptation of mysterious byways that lure us from our main-road duties?

At such moments we feel the earnestness of life and sense the onrush of time. We cannot linger undecided at the crossroads or stop too long by the wayside. Duty and decisions crowd urgently upon us. And every road taken is also a rejection of another.

Yet pale and past, the rejected roads linger always. The story of our life is more than the sum of our documented episodes and decisions. Modestly, behind the factual content of our life trail the unreal images of other roads we could have taken, other places we could have known, other lives we could have lived.

It is only in view of what we have said no to—and what has said no to us—that we can begin to make sense of human life, our own most of all. Historian Thomas Carlyle said that history does not reveal its alternatives. Perhaps not, but they remain in an ideal way nonetheless as lingering reminders of the magnitude of their sacrifices. The roads not taken, the chances missed, taken, or denied, are not mere nostalgic anecdotes of ancient renunciations but an abiding moral and explanatory justification of those we chose to follow. Each of us is a constellation of real and rejected lives. At varying distances from the dramatic center of our being, shining with faint or splendid luminosity, our chosen and forfeited ideals trace our way through the world. Paradoxically, who we are includes who we could not, or would not, be.

Article 2.
A Tale of Two Cities

I apply the title of Charles Dickens' novel to Athens and Jerusalem as symbols of the two cultures that have impacted Western civilization far more than the Paris and London featured in his famous book. Only a few hundred miles of Aegean and Mediterranean waters separated Athens and Jerusalem, yet so different were their cultures, histories and worldviews that it could almost be said that they represented different planets. Even though both cities still exist, I speak of them in the past tense because they began to lay the foundations of Western civilization nearly three thousand years ago.

In both cultures men sought knowledge and truth, but they went about it in very different ways. Jerusalem came to represent divinely revealed knowledge bestowed on those with an obedient and receptive spirit. On the other hand, Athens gave rise to an entirely new concept of knowledge: that which people may discover with human intellect.

Endowed with a unique religious genius, the Hebrews progressed beyond the polytheism of neighboring peoples to an enlightened vision of a single, almighty Creator and a cosmos rendered orderly by the just uniformity of his laws. As they understood it, all truth and power emanated from God, and the whole duty of man and the entire meaning of human life consisted in reverence and obedience.

The Athenian thinkers generally ignored popular Greek polytheism, taking care not to speak unfavorably against it and risk suffering the fate of Socrates. They had an intellectual concept of the divine but stopped far short of Hebrew religious intensity. Their passion was to use their intellect to discover the orderly consistency and behavior of the Cosmos, thus freeing themselves from superstitious dependence on unreliable signs and seers.

Both worldviews were destined to enrich and illuminate Western culture. To Jerusalem we trace the exalted concepts of brotherhood, charity, and the dignity and worth of the human person. And from Athens came a legacy of human rationality and an aesthetic appreciation of reality. Athens was the primal democracy and to it we return time and again for inspiration in governance and politics. Sainthood and spirituality had their roots in Jerusalem; disinterested scientific curiosity we get from Athens. Philosophy and mathematics developed in Athens; theology and the transcendent thought, in Jerusalem.

The West has alternated between the two visions, favoring first one, then the other. Every attempt to exclude one or the other has resulted in the impoverishment of the Western worldview. Theology cannot tell us how to build an airplane or explain quantum mechanics, but by its nature science is not suited to respond to the human hunger for ultimate meaning in life.

Ideally, it seems an immense advantage to preserve these dual legacies and the creative tension between them. At the moment the balance inclines to Athens, but when the need grows great, as it surely will, Jerusalem will no doubt reclaim its place, as it always has, and perhaps forever shall.

Article 3.
Pathetic Fallacy

In poetry a "pathetic fallacy" consists of attributing human emotions to non-human things—the moon, a flower, a sunset, and so on. But the same tendency also appears in other areas: gambling, weather, and even statistical prediction. Last summer I read that since we had not had a major hurricane since 2005, we were "dangerously overdue" for one. The statement was flawed on two counts. First, Hurricane Ike, which did massive damage in Houston, Galveston, and the Bolivar Peninsula, came ashore in 2008.

The second error was a human assumption—a pathetic fallacy—imposed on nature. We think that after trending for a long time in the same direction, pressure builds on cards, dice, statistics, and weather to make an "overdue" correction. But in nature there is no such pressure and nothing is ever "overdue." Nature and numbers have no memory of what happened before or concern for what will happen next. A gambler may be tied in emotional knots because he lost big on the previous roll of the dice, but the dice themselves are indifferent to his feelings. A coin toss is just as likely to come up heads again, even if it has done so fifty times in a row.

Of course, a major hurricane may occur not because it is overdue but because of natural phenomena. A panicky gambler may win or lose big on the next hand or roll of the dice. But it has nothing to do with the emotional disposition of numbers, cards, or dice, which know nothing and remember nothing. Impersonal things and forces do not keep score.

The gambler hopes to win, while the statistician tries to follow trends leading to accurate prediction. But in neither case is statistical evidence absolutely reliable. I recall that relying on statistical models storm forecasters predicted ten or twelve named storms in the Atlantic and Gulf in a recent year. There were no more than two or three. Events go awry and human behavior is notoriously unpredictable, as we saw in the Brexit vote and our recent elections.

If gamblers work on hunches and hopes, scientists rely on statistical probabilities. Both procedures may fail for similar reasons: unpredictable chance in the first, statistical variables that wander outside the paradigm in the second. And the shorter the time frame, the greater the unreliability. Science still enjoys general social respect, but emboldened by its prestige it appears with increasing frequency to risk its good name with predictions either based on faulty data or projected so far beyond their limits that they become mere guesswork.

So what conclusions can we draw from all this? Perhaps the realization that our present predictive methods are limited and must not be forced into areas where reasonable certainty is not yet possible. To do so in gambling is to risk losing our shirt. In scientific predictive analysis the loss may be even greater: the erosion of trust in the models and methodologies themselves.

Article 4: Inside the University

Someone wrote that universities reflect the general wellbeing or malaise of a nation. But they are hardly a microcosm of American society. Politically, American universities are much more liberal than the general populace. More than ninety percent of university professors classify themselves as such. There are exceptions in religious colleges and universities, but even in these schools many professors privately disregard official creeds and policies. But regardless of their politics, most dissenters choose to hide their inclinations. And with good reason; Machiavelli himself could learn from the exquisite forms of punishment meted out in the ivory towers of academe.

I smile when people tell me how fortunate I have been to work in a place without seamy politics. The university life is good, but politics there can be as nasty as anywhere else. Many professors believe they are the smartest people on earth and that no amount of money or honor is commensurate with what they deserve.

Yet practically all professors, left or right, are solid traditionalists when it comes to academic matters. Little has changed since the Middle Ages in the way students earn degrees. And the higher the degree, the more conservative the process. With rare exceptions, doctoral candidates must prove they are pedants before they become PhDs. Nearly all doctoral dissertations in the humanities and social sciences require copious footnotes or endnotes in the old European style. The content of these notes is often more pertinent than the text itself, though they render the work almost unreadable. But woe to students who dare say anything original! Normally, they can only cite what established scholars in the field have already said. The payoff for their pedantic servitude comes when younger scholars cite them. It means that they have joined the fraternity of experts.

Despite this archaic system, many students and professors consider it their duty to be social and political subversives. But there is a certain anxiety in their ranks these days due to the disappearance of glaring inequalities. They magnify those that remain to immeasurable dimensions, and if none is readily visible, may go on an underground search for new ones here or abroad. An unspoken rule on university campuses is that anything favorable to America is considered bad taste or the work of simpletons.

Regardless of this attitude, there is an obvious justification for these anti-establishment attitudes. One purpose of universities is to inject new ideas into public life. And new ideas usually have a disputatious history. Without them, social creativity tends to lag. A cause for great frustration among professors is that they have no public forum from which announce their ideas. The public pays little attention to their books and journals. Consequently, like unruly children, they sometimes go to intellectual and behavioral extremes so that the media will notice them.

For most of the students, the sobering demands of making a living soon moderate their radicalism. As philosopher George Santayana noted, despite the teachings by Harvard professors in his day, most students soon forgot their youthful subversions and became responsible citizens. For the majority of graduates today not much has changed.

Article 5.
A Brief History of Tolerance

It comes as no surprise that the Western concept of tolerance has religious roots. But not the sort we would expect if we compare tolerance to the iconic ideals of brotherhood, forgiveness, and charity. Early Christians were replete with these virtues, but they were unwilling to tolerate many things—Caesar-worship, gladiatorial death duels, and a bucket list of sins. Which explains why so many of them suffered martyrdom rather than yield.

On the other hand, the modern concept of tolerance had an inglorious beginning. It arose from the stalemate reached in the protracted religious wars of the sixteenth and seventeenth centuries between European Catholics and Protestants. The final outcome was not a consensual compromise but a realization by both weary sides that a definitive victory was not possible and that there was no choice but to acknowledge, that is, tolerate, the existence of the enemy.

In those portions of the world where the Western experience has not penetrated and does not resonate strongly, notions of religious and political tolerance are still in their infancy, if they exist at all. It is not uncommon for non-Westerners to look with incredulity on the Western idea that every conflict has two valid sides that may be mediated to the partial defeat and incomplete victory of both. To non-Westerners, truth as they see it, does not readily divide itself in two but separates itself cleanly from falsified versions. This is why they tend to see this willingness to accept opposing views and the willful defeat it signifies as a form of odd wrongheadedness that is either naïve or deceptive, or both. In any case, they look on sincerity as a minor virtue that has no place in power politics. This attitude may explain the mediocre record of Western diplomacy based on the sincere ideal of mutual tolerance.

Tolerance in all its forms presupposes opposites and oppositions, else it would have no purpose to begin with. And so it was in the struggles of the Reformation. These shook the foundations of what had been age-old, unquestioned beliefs and caused the worldview in which they were anchored to come apart at the cultural seams. Immemorial beliefs which had formed the deep, unconscious substructure of European life suddenly floated up to the level of collective awareness, weakening as they did so to ideas and becoming subject to debate, passion, hatred, and rejection.

The belief in tolerance differs from the idea of tolerance. Conscious toleration of other beliefs signifies that one's stated beliefs are no longer irrevocable but courteous and adjustable. In this regard, non-Westerners have glimpsed a truth that Westerners have not fully grasped. One's real beliefs, including the belief in tolerance, which operates at a subconscious level, are the subsoil of one's being that is too deep for conscious expression and manipulation.

Today tolerance is a mantra. How wrong would we be to say that we live under the tyranny of tolerance?

Article 6.
A choice of immortalities?

Ray Kurzweil, chief engineer at Google, Aubrey de Grey, biomedical gerontologist, and Aziz Aboobaker, University of Nottingham researcher are leaders in the quest for earthly immortality. Kurzweil himself is preparing to live forever. The only problem, he admits, is making sure he doesn't die before becoming immortal in twenty or thirty years. (Have you noticed how all the ideal things, like completing Houston road repairs, are always twenty or thirty years in the future?)

Consider some possibilities. One would be to transplant your brain into an artificial body. Think how it would affect the transgender controversy if you pranced into a dressing room in your unisex torso. Another way would be to repair our frayed telomeres and rebuild the old clunker of a body we already have. Many of us are already trying a variation of this approach. Have you noticed all the folks searching for youth restoratives or age preventatives in the herbal section at Walmart? Lately I'm suspicious. When a handsome twenty-five-year-old man or pretty woman walks by, I'm thinking they could really be my age but possessors of the secret formula. Maybe that's why some young people know everything: they were there when it happened.

For ages people had to die to live forever. Naturally there were some conditions attached, like loving a neighbor that you really wanted to hit upside the head, or being charitable when you secretly wanted to keep it all for yourself. Then there was that unpleasantness with hospitals, doctors, caskets, funerals, crying kinfolks, and enough flowers to cover Rhode Island. You got to smell the roses on your way out of this world while the community stayed to eat all the food in your house. (Nothing stimulates appetites like a funeral.)

If getting out of the world is a bother, living here forever might be a nightmare. Just think, you could be stuck with supporting worthless Uncle Bernard and ditzy Aunt Agnes for the next five hundred years. And on his 969th birthday your strung-out son announces that he's coming home to live—for the fortieth time. And since pensions and social security went the way of the dodo, what about having to start your 1000th career at age 1175? Then there are the daily riots by desperate unfortunates left off the immortality makeover list.

Yesterday a woman told me to "get a life." Her concern for me was touching, but I should have asked her where I could find one. Like Mr. Kurzweil, I may need a spare to make sure I last until the startup of manmade immortality. (If the future is anything like today, hardly anything but taxes will happen on time.)

On second thought, though, I think I'll just stay on the old, time-tested road to immortality. It worked for people a lot brighter and better than I am. Still, old habits die hard. You may still find me poking around the herbal section. Just in case.

Article 7:
A Fish out of Water

If we had never seen a fish and came upon one flopping on a shore, we might rationally conclude that its movements were senseless and absurd. But if we know that fish live in water and that this one was probably caught and abandoned by a fisherman, we can understand its desperate struggle to regain its aquatic environment. The fish's actions make sense once we know its natural circumstances and the probable history of how it came to be in its pathetic predicament.

So it is with human life. We begin to understand the actions of people and the course of their events when we see them emerge from a former situation, and that situation in turn from earlier ones. History is the story of why and how things and people came to be in their present situation and condition. Much, perhaps most, of what we call human nature is really human history. It is knowledge in its temporal depth and setting.

For centuries this historical understanding has competed at various levels with its rationalist alternative. Descartes (1596-1650) and his followers claimed that rational thinking alone was sufficient to understand the world and everything in it, including human reality. They argued that by exercising their rational minds Adam and Eve could access the same knowledge available to modern people.

Evaluating things only by their surface appearance, rationalists saw many things around them that appeared as senseless. Absurdity, satire, and dismissive attitudes toward the past became rationalist hallmarks. These culminated in

Voltaire's declaration that human history was little more than a chronicle of crime, injustice, and religious absurdity. Historical explanations did not interest the rationalists, an attitude that predisposed them to oppose traditional order and welcome revolutionary upheaval. The French Revolution soon followed.

The rationalist philosophers set out to abolish the historical understanding of cause and effect. Hume (1711-1776) wrote that the supposed link between the First Cause, or God, and the effect we know as the world is a mental habit without logical justification. In human affairs, Hume argued, the supposed effect could as easily be the cause.

Hegel (1770-1831) attempted to span the divide between history and rationalism by what he called "reason" in history. For Hegel, world history is the working out of an ultimate rational design by the Absolute Spirit. For his part, Marx (1818-1883) rejected the spirit but kept the design, which we know as communism.

In the twentieth century historical philosophy culminated in the view that history itself is the higher form of reason. It includes rationalist thought as a subset but surpasses it in scope. But if the historically focused philosophers were superior thinkers, the rationalists were better propagandists, which explains why so far they have prevailed. To the rationalists the claim that historical reason is superior to abstract rationalism still appears as absurd as a fish out of water.

Article 8: A Forgotten Genius

Few people have heard of Baltasar Gracián, yet at one time he was considered the genius of his age and one of the wisest thinkers of the second millennium. The great German philosopher Friedrich Nietzsche said of him, "Europe has never produced anything finer or more complicated in matters of moral subtlety." And the equally celebrated German thinker Arthur Schopenhauer wrote that "[his writing] is especially suited for the young who are intent on making their fortune. For to them it imparts in one and in advance the lessons which else they could derive only from protracted experience." Perhaps M.E. Grant Duff, Scottish administrator and Governor of Madras, paid Gracián the highest tribute: "Taking the book as a guide, I have never chanced to meet with anything which seemed to me even distantly to approach it."

Gracián was a Spanish Jesuit, counselor to kings, philosopher and novelist in Spain's two-century-long Golden Age of art, empire and literature (1474-1681). Born in the Kingdom of Aragon in 1601, he died near his birthplace in 1658 after holding professorial positions. He suffered considerably at the hands of superiors resentful and fearful of his intellect, and was often in hot water for his writings, which were not always properly sanctioned by the Church. His controversial "Letter from Hell" is typical.

His ideas have the diamantine brilliance and intensity found in other classic works such as Machiavelli's *The Prince* and Sun-Tzu's *The Art of War*. Hear samplings of his maxims: "The shortest road to being 'somebody' is knowing who to follow."

"Useless discussions never lead to useful decisions." "Think twice, speak once." "To concede today may be the best way to succeed tomorrow." "The need to release frustration makes a perfectly pleasant man a lamentable bore." "A maxim for the wise: leave before being left." "The path of the wise is to seek the wiser." "He who is self-reliant, when carrying himself, carries everything with him." "When you reach the pinnacle of your industry or art, beware of underlings. Certain information should be withheld from those who may seek to replace you. Learn to keep the ultimate refinements of your specialty to yourself." "Never allow the obligation to exceed what can be repaid; nothing will lose more friends than to place them in too heavy debt." "Beware of those mired in misfortune who call to you for comfort. These men are on the hunt for those who will help them carry their baggage." "Never participate in the secrets of those above you. You think you are privileged to share the fruit, but you also may be sharing the pits and the rind, and you run the risk of being eaten."

Although Spain remained a power until the nineteenth century, other nations surpassed it. Its decline eclipsed the fame of several worthy Spaniards. Some of these are only now being rediscovered, foremost among them the brilliant Jesuit thinker Baltasar Gracián.

Article 9:
A Touch of Religious Sociology

Religious imperialism has been one of the great catalysts of history. By persuasion or force rival religions have periodically reshuffled civilizations in their quest to convert all humanity to their respective faiths.

But in the convoluted manner of modern times, other groups have now arisen whose aim is not to win converts but to rid the world of religion altogether. For these persons, mostly former Christians concentrated in Europe and the English-speaking countries, religion has ceased to be a dimension of their life. Why this hostility to religion in the very countries where Christianity has had its greatest success?

Perhaps partly for this very reason. The Christianized West has come closer than any other culture to creating the worldly paradise that the old utopians promised but could not deliver. Today the average Western person enjoys wonders of transportation, housing, food, education, entertainment, and communications that the greatest kings could not dream of in former times. Today we think no more of these marvels than the air we breathe.

There were no remedies for poverty, disease, and early death in former times. Today we look on these not as fate but as social injustices and demand solutions. And many believe that in a few decades medical science will be able to prolong life and health indefinitely. Life here and now in this world was never more attractive.

All this caused several adjustments in religious views of the next life. Darwinism and modern science persuaded countless people that far from being created in the image of God, himself often dismissed as a metaphorical fable, man was simply another animal, a clever primate destined to live, die, and dissolve into constituent elements. Earlier mankind believed the Hereafter would be infinitely better than this earthly sojourn, but now in comparison to modern life with its comforts and cures, the next life seems less appealing. Let's be honest: we feel sorry for the dead as they depart this full life for a realm where marriage, sex, food, drink, sports, and pets may not exist.

Where does this leave us today? For a start, with the need to rethink whether human life really conforms to the perishable Darwinian model—a possibility—or is instead a higher form of life destined to survive in a much richer realm—also a possibility that needs thought. Science claims to have settled the matter in Darwin's favor. But all human things must be revisited and rethought. Truth does not change, but we do, and in recent years this change has resulted in new perspectives of human reality that could challenge and reverse the earlier rush to judgment. We have no way of knowing the effect, if any, these new views will have on traditional religion and conventional science but the possibilities are fascinating.

Article 10:
All Women Were Beautiful

Russian novelist Dostoyevsky wrote that all women were already half beautiful just by being women. But on the Texas frontier of 1842 Mrs. S.L. Shipe went him one better when she declared: "Ugliness availed nothing, for woman's minority was so great that plainness of feature had lost its significance and all women were beautiful."

Accounts from that period mention the scarcity of marriageable women. Competition for wives meant that men could not be picky. No woman was condemned to spinsterhood and remained single only if she so chose, and younger widows especially had ample opportunities to remarry. Some women married while still in their early teens. Dilue Rose Harris married at thirteen, but demographic records from 1850 show that most brides were in their late teens or early twenties, while the average for men was twenty-six. Probably these statistics were also true of the Republic era.

If chances for marriage were "the best of times," in the words of novelist Charles Dickens, the hardships of frontier life and the regularity of pregnancies also made marriage "the worst of times" for many Texas women. Numerous pregnancies were burdensome and dangerous, and some women tried to interrupt them. One woman confided to her sister: "And so you are going ahead of me in the multiplication line. Am I free yet? Yes!! No more babies for me . . . I must not exult too much, I might be caught yet; but I'll try not." She does not say how she prevented or interrupted pregnancies, but some methods reportedly were more dangerous than the pregnancies themselves. These included violent exercise or "strong blows to the belly," "Seneca snakeroot," and savin, the extract of juniper berries. It is worth noting that the moral issues associated with abortion today did not exist in the early nineteenth century. The fetus was not considered to be alive until the "quickening," that is, the time when the mother could feel it move or kick. The ignorance of the reproductive process was remarkable; until the late 1840s, even doctors had human fertility patterns reversed. Euphemisms for pregnancy reflected an extraordinary prudishness: "taking the cold" "in a family way," "she is larger," "I don't think it all fat," or "her fat will fall in her arms." Other than with their husbands, many women did not speak of pregnancy at all when other men—including their sons—were present. Mary Maverick, who had ten children, referred to one of her pregnancies as ". . . a trial and hardship incident to our love."

In addition to running their households and caring for numerous children, frontier women were charged with educating their offspring, and in a larger sense, their communities. They were called the "sweet civilizers" and "gentle tamers," and far more than the tough marshals of later Hollywood fame were responsible for eventually toning down violence, drunkenness, and lawlessness and imposing order, manners, and decorum on rough and tumble frontier Texas.

Article 11: Old Sayings

America was old before it was young. Between the founding of Jamestown in 1607 and the declaration of American independence in 1776 Americans were still English and were not allowed west of the Appalachian Mountains. Their English origin showed in their customs, speech, and place names. Virginia, Carolina, Georgia, Maryland, Jersey, York, Hampshire, and Baltimore were among hundreds of names brought over from old England. With notable exceptions—Massachusetts, for instance—they used relatively few native place names until they reached trans-Appalachian regions—Kentucky, Tennessee, Ohio, Alabama, Mississippi, Illinois, Texas, and Iowa among others. Further west and south they incorporated Spanish names—Florida, California, Los Angeles, San Antonio, Santa Fe, El Paso, Colorado, and some French: Baton Rouge, Des Moines, Terre Haute, Saint Louis.

As Americans moved west, their English became more creative. Today American English produces more new words, both technical and slang, than any other English-speaking country. But Americans also preserve many archaic features, especially in pronunciation. Oddly enough, the oldest versions of languages are often found in the newest countries. One hears in Mexico, Central America and other Hispanic countries old Spanish vocabulary that has disappeared in Spain itself. The same is generally true of Canadian French, Brazilian Portuguese, and American English.

Many of these older forms are preserved in folk sayings. "I ain't hyeard" (I haven't heard), is an Appalachian expression meaning I don't know, a response to the question how far is it to such and such a place. Similar expressions lingered in England until the nineteenth century. "Without a sound shoe to his foot," meant a man without money or resources. "A woman of her tonnage," an unkind reference to a sizable woman. "She's getting to be husband-high," meant a girl nearly old and tall enough to be married. (Girls in old England and America usually married at a tender age.) "She'll wish her cake dough afore she's done of him," meaning she'll regret marrying him. "Do you mind when we were young and carefree?" "Mind" also meant remember in older English. "But daze me if I ever see a man wait so long before he take so little," said of an old bachelor who marries a woman not only plain looking but poor besides. "When the pigs be many, the wash runs thin," said of a family with many children and little food in the house. Thomas Hardy, English author of *Tess of the d'Ubervilles* includes many such expressions in his novels. "He looks like a man with corns that's walked all day in tight boots" was said in old Texas said of a man with miseries showing in his face.

Oddly enough, American English is arguably closer in pronunciation to the language of Shakespeare than the typical British version one hears in stage productions. In 1776 both the Redcoats and the Revolutionaries spoke with essentially the same accent. The sounds we associate with British English were not fully developed until the nineteenth century.

Article 12: Apocalypse Everywhere

"Apocalypse" is an emotionally charged Greek word that sends a shiver through us. In English it means "revelation," the title of St. John the Divine's last book of the Bible. Many people find his prophecies terrifying, but others hope for their fulfillment. Early Christians believed the world would end soon. It did not, but the expectation remained, leading to countless false predictions. In the year 1ooo, for instance, people were so convinced the world was about to end that they abandoned their homes and climbed to mountain tops to await the cosmic consummation. Not until the date passed uneventfully and people sheepishly came down from the mountains did Europeans get busy building cathedrals and preparing for a longer earthly stay. Most of us remember the milder panic a thousand years later in 2000.

Today this apocalyptic outlook is not limited to religion. Hollywood has made a cliché of worldwide devastation, usually linking it to invading aliens. (I note, however, that even as the world is exploding, there is never a shortage of bullets to shoot aliens, vehicles to blow up, and gasoline to fuel them.)

Some economists are predicting the apocalyptic collapse of the dollar and the markets, and books about the catastrophic demise of civilization have been standard fare of publishing houses for nearly a century. Then there are the scientific predictions that the world will either overheat, freeze over, die from poisonous pollution, or blow itself up. Years ago a scientist showed a group of us a replica of the "doomsday clock" and declared the inevitable mutual destruction of the USA and the USSR. The clock hands were only two minutes from midnight and creeping ever closer to the fatal hour. Yet midnight never came. Chance sometimes trumps certainty.

But if these calamities are not enough to finish us off, pandemics may do the job. And should we run short of doomsday scenarios, within a few billion years, they tell us, the sun will expand into a red giant and incinerate the earth, or Andromeda, our sister galaxy, now speeding towards us, will collide with the Milky Way and pulverize our solar system.

What are we make to make of all these apocalyptic scenarios? Two things occur to me. The first is Ralph Waldo Emerson's belief that "a deep remedial force" is at work in creation. The world is more resilient than we know. The second is the admission that indeed the world could end today for a combination of reasons, divine, cosmic, and human. But since individually we have no control over most of them, only somewhat over ourselves, would it not be wiser of us to do less handwringing over things beyond our power and put our personal house in order to be ready for two possibilities: a world that could end today or one that may endure for ages to come.

Article 13: Baby Talk

Scientists tell us that only one human species still exists in the world. But anybody with any life experience knows there are at least two: babies and grownups.

Because we are different human species, it is hard for us to communicate. Babies don't know our language and we have forgotten theirs.

Even if they knew grownup language, we don't speak it with babies. Instead we resort to a kind of "baby babble," which nobody understands. If babies could understand it, they probably would dismiss grownups as oversize morons. Maybe they do anyway. Of course, "baby babble" is not meant to convey information, only adoration. With all this against them, it's a wonder babies ever learn grownup language at all.

Meanwhile, all they can do is cry as a way to control the big beings they use as beasts of burden and food providers. Unperceptive grownups such as fathers or siblings may scream back at them in frustration. Only a loving mother, herself a temporary returnee to the baby universe, understands their angry or anguished cries.

If you doubt the differences between these two species I am describing, just take a look at babies. They hardly resemble us at all. Their heads are far too big for their bodies and their hands and feet too small and soft for practical uses. Arms, legs, and torso are also of disproportionate lengths.

Babies are rude, totally lacking in table manners and potty protocols. Instead of the polite platitudes we say to strangers we meet, babies are more likely to scream in fear or disgust at the sight of huge faces twisted by the terrifying grimaces called smiles. We still have not decided definitively whether babies are only a notch lower than angels or a rung higher than chimpanzees.

If babies perceive we pose no threat to them, they may put us on trial, staring unblinkingly into our eyes and reading our character with a wisdom that was already old when the stars were young. Their judgment is absolute and without appeal. We feel an inward tremor as we await their verdict, boastfully happy if they smile at us, secretly troubled by self-doubts if they cry in fear.

Because a baby's joy is serious, it is genuine. Years will pass before it begins to supplement lagging happiness with humor.

Theirs is the serious joy of astonishment. Babies fascinate because they are fascinated by the mere magic of creation. For us the enchantment we once knew ourselves may have faded into the humdrum light of a latter day. As the poet says, "there hath passed away a glory from the earth." Our recompense and reason are now of a lower order.

But the world does not end with our adult doubts and dreads. It is not one and done with our doings. Such finalities are not ours to call. Instead, it could be that in each baby's life, in any one of those oversize little heads "the world's great age begins anew. The golden years return."

Article 14:
Aliens on a Texas Beach

There they lay: four little aliens half buried in the sand where the children tossed them as they raced, screaming happily, toward their beach house and impatient parents. No, these miniature plastic beings were not from Mars or a galaxy far, far away but from a country called China. Now they waited in suspended violence for the children to come back and resume the war to save the Universe.

Their wait may be long, perhaps forever, I thought. The children may not return at all. The packed family car and angry father probably meant the end of their summer vacation. Maybe they will come back next year when they have forgotten this war and, a year older, prefer to play with more sophisticated toys. It takes enormous imagination to animate the aliens and give them life, story, and purpose. And as this gift fades with age we need more complex playthings to entertain us.

I pick up one of the aliens and try my hand at play. I aim its menacing weapon at a darting sandpiper, but there is no thrill. Maturity has reduced me to mere materiality. I see only cheap plastic and think of environmental clutter and trade imbalances, things vastly unworthy of childhood.

Childhood is a treasury soon depleted. Quickly we use up the world, burning away its halo of higher realms—the truer kingdom of magic and miracles—leaving only the lowest, crudest rung of creation we call reality. We once held dominion over a brighter world that still echoes in music, art, and play, but most of us have forgotten the reentry code.

Yet childhood, seemingly so quickly gone, is not really short. We forget that it is nearly an eternity, another species of time vast and meaningful beyond telling. It is a paradox, but bright and happy like many things close to the Divine.

Not again in our mature years shall we enjoy so close a fellowship with happiness nor possess again so much world and time for ourselves.

Yet we long to grow up, eager to learn the way of the world. But for this knowledge we must barter the higher truths and the greater insight we mistakenly call innocence.

I walk down the beach to my own destiny, wondering whether the children will return to gather up the aliens. No, for now I see the carrier-laden car drive away. Probably the children have forgotten about the aliens. For them life is too full and immediate for clinging memories. Their eternity is compressed into an endless now. The poet Blake said it better: "To hold infinity in the palm of your hand. And eternity in an hour."

Perhaps tomorrow other children will claim the tiny aliens for other games. We build our life with realities that migrate through many lives. Things have no everlasting loyalty to us but lend themselves only for a season. And wisdom, we learn at last, lies in using them well and releasing them with grace and gratitude when our short lease expires.

Shore and surf, original metaphors of life, turn us to transcendent thoughts. Seashores make philosophers of us all. We cannot decipher the meaning of the deeper currents, yet we know, as it was in the beginning, that in its rise and ebb the tide marks the rhythm of the world. Injured by imbalances, we come here hoping to restore harmonies and find a cure for melancholy. The splendor of creation washes over our skepticism and in a joyous complicity deeper than we know unites us anew with the happy, heroic children who save the Universe from evil for yet another day.

The seashore is dense with the destiny of all things, even four forgotten little aliens half buried on a Texas beach.

Article 15:
View from a Mississippi Window

I looked out my Mississippi motel window and saw what I expected to see: a grove of pines, scattered oaks, and golden sage grass in the open spaces. It was old familiar reality. Or was it? What if some great cosmic Deceiver is filling my head with false images? How can I be sure, how can anybody be sure, that the pine grove, oaks, and grasses are really there as they appear to be?

Common sense tells me that I can walk out among the trees and grasses, touch them, and maybe bump into a limb or trip over a root. It is hard to doubt a stubbed toe.

But common sense covers only common things, and the world is full of strange things beyond its reach, for example, the way things seem to shrink with distance. An optical illusion, but where is the boundary between illusion and reality?

French philosopher René Descartes (1596-1650) asked the same questions and came up with this answer: I can be sure of only one truth: *I think, therefore I am*. Everything else he left to "systematic doubt." Modern European philosophy was built on this famous premise.

But his celebrated premise proved to be a prison. It was like being in a sealed room lined with mirrors. Everywhere you looked you saw only your own reflection, your own mind. There seemed to be no way out. And out to what? The world outside the mind was still anybody's guess. For centuries the Who's Who of European philosophy—Leibniz, Kant, Husserl—remained in Descartes' sealed room, speculating brilliantly about the elusive "thing-in-itself" outside the mind. Finally, in

1927, a philosopher escaped this mental confinement and introduced a new way of thinking about reality. Claiming that the formula, *I think, therefore I am*, was the basic premise of philosophy went too far—or maybe not far enough. He reasoned simply that in order to think at all there must be real things to think about. In order to see, I must have before me actual things to see. Otherwise, I could not think at all, could not see at all, and by Descartes own formula, could not be at all.

A new paradigm then emerges: Reality consists not of "things in themselves," nor of me imprisoned in my mind. Instead it is I with real things and real people, acting with them, an activity we call living. He put it this way: "I am I and my circumstance, and if I do not save it, I do not save myself." Things and I are both real, as common sense always told us we were, but we are real together, not in isolation.

The thinker who broke the Cartesian paradox was Spanish philosopher Ortega y Gasset (1883-1955). He made many other philosophical advances, but for two reasons few European and American philosophers know anything about him. First, he wrote in Spanish, which hardly any philosophers knew in those times, and second, few of his writings have been translated, and many drably so.

Not that Ortega, as he was called, was an unknown thinker. He wrote *The Revolt of the Masses* (1927), a sensational international bestseller translated into all major Western languages. Today his prophetic insights are chilling and more relevant than ever.

Ortega paid a price for his genius. Conservatives, Marxists, radical Republicans, the Press, the government, the universities, and powerful Church factions all reviled him.

He spent years in exile, plagued by health and financial problems. But immune to all ideologies, he ignored his enemies, producing to the end works full of truth and beauty.

Ortega taught me many things, among them how better to understand the view from a Mississippi window half a world away.

Article 16:
Stopped at a Red Light

As I sit in my car waiting for the red light to change, it occurs to me that in some ways we have less freedom than our forefathers had. For example, I am forced to pay a state agency for license plates for this car even though that shadowy entity paid not a dime toward its purchase. Then there's inspection, insurance, and taxes I must pay even though the car, supposedly, belongs exclusively to me. Think how perplexed and outraged our ancestors would have been had there been similar requirements for their wagons and oxcarts.

We pay taxes on both sides of the road but unless we live in left-handed places like Great Britain, we must drive only in the right lanes. But our ancestors, like the fabled chicken, could cross to the other side in their wagons any time they took a notion. And the list of such legal requirements goes on. Seat belts, size requirements and placement for children's car seats, speed limits and school zones, proper lights, and of course stop signs and red lights. And all this applies only to automobiles.

Outside our cars we must comply with a labyrinth of laws and rules about nearly every aspect of our lives. Think of multiple tax levels, compulsory school attendance and inoculations; required social security numbers and birth certificates; licenses and fees for nearly everything imaginable, ordinances about garbage pickup and prohibitions against trash burning, overgrown lawns, free-roaming pets, and deed restrictions about what we can and cannot build on our property. Even dying is a complicated legal matter. I read some time back that the Chinese authorities have outlawed reincarnation. It's expensive to be here now and—in China at least—illegal to come back.

I can hear you reminding me that laws, taxes, prohibitions, ordinances, and legalities are necessary in order to have an orderly and humane society. True, I grant you, but how much is too much? Every year councils, legislators, congresses, and agencies from Walla Walla to Washington enact more laws and regulations for us to obey. There is a compulsions in officials, elected or appointed, to fix things, broken or not, and to pass ordinances because—well because that's what we elect them to do.

Taking a broader view, I also hear you proudly reminding me that our modern democracies have greatly expanded our rights. You are right. Our modern democratic governments are immensely more powerful and efficient than the puny monarchies of earlier centuries. When Louis XVI of France boasted, "I am the State," he was essentially telling the truth. The State didn't amount to very much else in those simple times.

I am simpleminded about politics, but tell me, isn't there a difference between rights and freedoms? It bothers me that a constitutional government can grant us rights because it means that we don't possess them already. When a government fails—and don't they all fail sooner or later?—our rights vanish with them. Besides, if they can give with one hand, can't they take back with the other? And does it seem to you that the more rights we win the more freedom we lose?

At one thing seems clear: neither our rights nor our freedoms are real unless we are brave enough to activate them. Fearful folks are never free, and we have only the freedoms and rights we dare to exercise. We say we have freedom of speech, for example, but aren't most of us too timid to say what we really think, especially in polite—make that timid—society? And probably a good thing too. What a jungle society would be if we spoke as bravely in public as we do in private! One of the first things we learn as children is what we can and cannot say. The long hand of the law goes only so far in its punishment; a parent's hand goes much farther. But the light is green and the law says I must go on.

Article 17: Death Row

Debates about American "exceptionalism" divide along familiar left/right political fault lines. I leave those arguments to others. But there is one case of American exceptionalism we can all agree on: we are exceptionally fat.

Recently I spent time in Spain and Colombia. In both countries food is plentiful and delicious, and friends all but stood in line to invite me to one tasty meal after another. I ate three full meals a day, more than I do at home. Yet I returned a few pounds lighter but shocked by so many overweight Americans. Obesity does not discriminate; all races are eligible. Colombians and Spaniards have an enviable diet, yet I saw no obese people in either country, and only one moderately overweight person who, it turned out, had lived in Austin. So what is going on? How can people in other nations eat well and stay trim? More to the point, what is making us Americans so fat?

You may say people are slender in those countries because they walk a lot. Not the case; they depend on automobiles as much as we do, and if you doubt it, Houston-sized traffic jams in the major cities will convince you otherwise.

I suspect our "fat" problem is linked to what I call "Death Row." No, I'm not referring to prison executions but to supermarket aisles. They may be some of the most dangerous places in America. Come with me down the aisle as I explain my suspicions.

Here we are in the bread section. I pick up a loaf of wheat bread and check it for ingredients and additives. Thirty-seven, that's right, thirty-seven, many of them unpronounceable and familiar only to a chemist: calcium iodate, calcium peroxide, thoxylated mono-and diglycerides, enzymes, stearoyl lactylate, azodicarbonamide, and the list goes on.

Does anybody really know the synergistic effects of all the added chemicals, preservatives, hormones, and genetically modified ingredients in our food? The FDA assures us they are harmless. Perhaps, but then we read that nearly half the FDA budget comes from pharmaceutical companies they regulate. Not a great confidence-builder.

What we do know is that something—like the witch in the story of Hanzel and Gretel—is fattening us up for the kill.

Doctors tell us obesity is the opening act of a tragically unfolding health drama. Drs. Michael Roizen and Mehmet Oz wrote recently in the Daily News that obesity causes permanent gene changes that are passed on to offspring. It takes the children of overweight mothers longer to feel full, so naturally they eat more.

Not many of us read medical journals. If we did, perhaps we would discover that cancer, Alzheimer's, Parkinson's, obesity, and other conditions—some never heard of until recently—seem to be getting worse with no real cures in sight.

The main difference I detect between our food and the normal diet of countries like Spain, Colombia, and others is a witch's brew of foreign ingredients added to our processed food: colorings, preservatives, artificial sweeteners, trans- fats, syrups, animal growth hormones, genetically altered plants, and others.

We have to wonder if some of these additives stimulate appetites to uncontrollable levels. For not even radical stomach surgeries work in many cases. Several persons I know regain their weight beginning with only a third of their original stomach. In a few years they are obese again, only now with additional health problems.

At the moment we have no real solution to the problem. Obesity rules in America, and like our waistline, its domain keeps expanding.

Article 18:
Depths and Superficialities

When I was a young professor it puffed up my vanity to hear my students say things like "Wow, that's really deep!" Today it would sadden me to hear such comments, for they would remind me that I had failed as a teacher.

But no question about it, deep ideas impress us and nobody wants to be labeled "superficial." Later, about the time I was plodding my way through Martin Heidegger's *Sein und Zeit* [Being and Time], it occurred to me that we have things upside down in these modern times. When done right, philosophy becomes, or ought to become, a superficial matter. Let me explain what I mean.

Things are shy and like to hide themselves in depth and darkness, as the old saying reminds us, we can't see the forest because it lies hidden behind the trees. For this reason the Heideggers of this world have no choice but to dive into the depths, as expert divers dive for pearls in some Far Eastern countries. But the next step, often omitted, is even more important: they must bring up these pearls of wisdom, science, or art from the depths to the surface, the superficies, so that we can see and learn about them in the light of day. It is not the thinker's duty to connive with the darkness by plunging us also into the depths, much less to leave us there.

Things hidden in the depths become knowable only as they emerge on the surface where they reveal form, shape, and structure, in a word, order. And order is compatible with the mind, the compatibility we call reason, understanding, and knowledge.

But there is a catch. As things emerge from the depths and assume an orderly spacing and structure that we can understand and manipulate to one degree or another, they also hide other things behind or below them. Every discovery or revelation becomes in turn a further concealment and a clue to deeper mysteries, every enlightenment hints of further darkness. This is why the pursuit of learning, knowledge, and understanding is an endless task. There are always more pearls in the depths.

Ironically, then, we can say that knowledge and understanding involve the general art of superficiality, the art of bringing unknown, hidden things to the surface so that we can understand them with ordinary intelligence.

Superficial does not mean shallow. In fact, they are diametrically opposed. By definition shallowness is the absence of depth, whereas the superficial must have depth in order to be a surface in the first place. Science, theology, poetry, literature, art, music, and architecture in their many forms all aim to bring things from the depths into the light so that we may understand and appreciate them. Michelangelo saw David trapped inside a rough marble block and freed him from his deep prison so he could shine forth as a great masterpiece. When done right, philosophy performs a similar task.

Article 19: Going in Circles?

Several philosophers of history, among them Comte and Marx, saw history as a series of inevitable cultural or economic stages. We call these doctrines determinism, which is a nineteenth-century rebranding of ancient fatalism and secular cousin to varieties of religious predestination. Applied to nations, it is the theory that they cannot deviate from a predetermined course. Determinism is typical of old, autumnal civilizations afflicted with historical arthritis.

As a younger nation whose cultural joints are still flexible, we Americans have never bought deeply into these creaky doctrines. Most of us are hard at work in the belief that destiny is ours to shape or squander.

But are we wrong? Is America following a preset pathway that will become evident as our society grows older? Despite some repeating similarities suggestive of a swinging pendulum, there is more evidence of rotating gradations of history. Let me illustrate.

Prudish Victorians and Puritans have alternated with bawdy counterparts in the long history of Great Britain. According to scholar Urban T. Holmes, single mothers accounted for nearly half of all births in medieval Scotland. In Queen Elizabeth's "spacious days" the English were notorious for drunken rowdiness. Eighteenth-century London teemed with alehouses, drunks, prostitutes, thieves, and starving children.

In 98 AD, Roman historian Tacitus described the primitive Germans as ferocious tribes who would fight to the death rather than submit to Roman law, which they saw as an infringement on their personal freedom. But this *Furor Teutonicus*, or Teutonic Fury, as the Romans called it, alternated in later times with discipline and obedience to authority.

Closer to home, concepts that Americans enthusiastically embraced in the nineteenth century—imperialistic expansion, environmental exploitation, assumptions of cultural and racial superiority—are embarrassments today.

These examples suggest that instead of a pendulum, a better metaphor of history is a giant wheel like an unstoppable Hindu juggernaut on which the vices and virtues of one era appear to rotate by degrees to become their polar opposites. Strapped to the great wheel rolling at different speeds according to the culture, the lofty descends by degrees to the lowly while the forbidden rises to become the favored. But unlike the swinging pendulum that does not progress, a wheel rolls forward in its rotations, which means that history never repeats because of new circumstances.

If the wheel of history keeps rolling, what does it portend for America's future? For a possible answer, think of notable American traits—optimism, democracy, charity, enterprise—then imagine a society where their opposites prevail. Years ago I wrote pessimistically that if America turned dictatorial, it would be the mightiest oppressive country in history. (I was young, and the young enjoy pessimism.)

Yet even then I knew that the old determinists overlooked something in their rigid paradigms: unpredictable chance, Providence's ace in the hole. Just when the world seems destined to roll on forever along a preset course, the wheels fall off, the pattern breaks, and humanity is free to begin again.

Article 20:
A Matter of Words

In American English several overworked adjectives divide roughly according to age brackets. People over fifty tend to describe the completion of any routine task as "a *tremendous* job" or praise a man who may be the merest mediocrity by calling him "a *tremendous* guy." *Desperate* is sometimes interchangeable with *tremendous* if exertion or fear is involved, as in a *desperate* or *tremendous* leap to catch a pass or a *desperate* effort to remember a wife's birthday. The younger generations overwork their own set of words, labeling ordinary people or events as *"awesome"* or *"cool."* Can anyone still remember when *"swell"* was the "cool" word of its time?

So what's the point? Who needs many words when three or four will cover the descriptive spectrum? Consider some ideas on the matter.

Language is the treasury of human potential and like all human things, it must be learned, which means it may also be lost. Think of the rich emotional nuances and verbal beauty that vanished from our culture when lyric poetry disappeared. Our relationships, particularly emotional ones, are cruder and less expressive without it, and cruder and less expressive means less human.

Despite the myth, common in college courses, that all languages are equal and equally expressive, some are so limited that they permit only the simplest mental options. We cannot conceive what we cannot say in words or convey with symbols. Think of trying to teach complex mathematics in a society ignorant of decimals, division, multiplication, and algebraic reasoning, or relativity theories to people convinced that ancestral spirits control the Cosmos.

The rise of civilization nearly always parallels the perfection of language. Originally Latin was the simple speech of farmers and shepherds. At its classical apogee when Rome ruled much of the known world, it was a marvel of precision and beauty in Horace and Cicero. Cervantes and Calderón wrote their masterpieces in the Golden Age of Spain. English power and culture soared with Shakespeare and Milton. French predominance peaked with language perfected under Racine and Molière.

Similarly, the demise of civilizations generally coincides with the decline of language. Less than three centuries after Rome fell Latin had already splintered into the rough ancestral dialects of the Romance Languages. It would take centuries for them to develop into the modern instruments they are today.

As languages decline, so historically do human learning and creativity. Which occurs first? Hard to say; they seem to happen together. Humanity advances and regresses in successive peaks and valleys of brilliance and dullness, both of which are mirrored in the richness or poverty of language.

But there is another element to keep in mind. Like all human attributes, language can be used or abused. With it we impart knowledge and describe truth and beauty. But with it also we may lie, slander, and defame. The difference is ethical discipline, the master component of human intelligence.

Article 21: Cultural Downsizing?

We hear a lot these days about cultural decline: students who can't learn, adults who can't read, and a general "dumbing down" of the population. Millions of people have almost no knowledge of science, history, art, literature, and religion. If our culture were a person, it would be flat lining on its deathbed.

Nobody is happy about the mess and everybody has their favorite political ogres to blame for the perceived decline. No need to name the usual suspects here. But before we toss in the cultural towel, consider a few points that get little attention.

First, after teaching for over fifty years, I'll let you in on a little secret. There have always been students who couldn't learn and people who couldn't tell you which hemisphere the USA was in, much less find it on a map. Illiteracy, which was normal for adult Americans two centuries ago, was—and is— still fairly common

But educational deficiencies are only part of the educational scene. I began noticing another phenomenon several decades ago. The brightest students of today are brighter than the best students of my day. I say it without condescension. Are we dividing into two Americas: the super smart and the super slow? It is an enigma for social scientists and a nightmare for teachers.

Naturally, we pin our future hopes on the bright students. But don't give up on the slow ones just yet. Our universities turn out intellectual specialists in every cultural field, but intellectuals usually do not save nations in times of crisis. That chore goes to plain people whose knowledge is limited but their courage is not. Intellectuals—bless their little pointy heads—are more likely to undermine national resolve.

Culture has several definitions. In the broadest sense we can describe it as a general repertory of concepts, methodologies, and technologies for solving problems, defining values, and enhancing lives.

But at times parts of the cultural field, or canon, outlive their purpose and become excess baggage. This is true in academic culture, which I know best. Much of it has become too unwieldy to assimilate.

Hundreds of unreadable books clog the different fields. Thousands of pointless articles are a wearisome burden for the student. Bibliographical entries serve not so much to help the reader as to highlight the erudition of the writer.

Occasionally we have to slough off parts of adipose culture, as frontier Americans simplified top-heavy European civilization and created the lean, adaptable culture destined to revolutionize the world several times over.

Cultural downsizing and streamlining seems to be happening again. If so, then the bright youngsters popping up in increasing numbers may refocus culture in a more usable way.

Is that usable, trimmed-down model a certainty? Not at all, but neither are the doomsday predictions we hear almost daily. As always, it is up to us to make the best or worst of alternatives the world presents. Either way, we stand to lose many things, good and bad. History is clear on the matter: some things have to end so that others can begin.

Article 22: Love, Marriage, and Some Consequences

You can hate just about anybody you please and nobody really cares. It's when you start loving people that you get into trouble. Love conquers all, so the old saying goes. Perhaps, but some kinds of love can also get you killed. Think of religious martyrs and murdered spouses. A husband usually doesn't mind if his wife hates the man next door, but Heaven help her if she should fall in love with him. The same erotic love that for modern people is the fulfillment of life was to the ancient Greeks a divine curse destined to end in tragedy.

Regardless of age differences and other factors, there is a normal attraction between the sexes. Usually nothing comes of it, but when the latent attraction veers towards love, it needs channels and limits to allow it to mature and stabilize within controllable boundaries.

The lengthy, orchestrated courtship of former times was a means of cultivating and humanizing the tidal wave of emotions that love arouses. But now that society has either altogether dispensed with courtship or severely curtailed it, many people immediately begin physical intimacy. This experience, like picking green fruit, stunts the emotions before they mature into enduring, bonded love.

Marriages based on this amorous immaturity are eggshell fragile and divorce is epidemic. We read that both the numbers and percentages of unmarried persons in American society have reached an all-time high. If marriage were a hospital patient, it would probably be in intensive care.

But so what? What's wrong with being single if marriage doesn't work out?

For many people nothing. Marriage is not for everyone. Because of personal and professional singularities some people thrive in solitude, and those who dread being alone usually make the worst companions.

On the other hand, social engineers who still claim that the family is the basic unit of society believe quite logically that marriages and families are necessary to hold society together. This obviously is not true; if it were, society would be in its agony. Far from being the building blocks of society, families are our refuge and escape from the social world. Impersonal society ends at the threshold where personal family life begins.

For this reason whether people are married or single has little to do with the impersonal forces we call society. If anything, the decline of marriage and the rise of singles expand society by obligating unmarried people to spend more of their life in public and social arenas, taking unshared responsibility for business decisions, relationships, shopping, selling, taxes, health matters, entertainment, and the like.

An unexamined consequence of the loveless life is a noticeable indifference toward the next life and a corresponding decline of religion. If one does not love in this life, what real incentive is there to live in the next? This need not be a strident denial of an afterlife, merely a passive lack of interest in it and a weary willingness to let it all come to a close in the nothingness of death.

Article 23: Middle-aged Teens?

In Europe recently I was in the company of several young professional men and women. From their trim, youthful looks and the things they talked about—restaurants, clubs, movies, beaches, parties, and bed partners du jour—I thought they were in their twenties. I was shocked to learn that several were almost forty. Some still lived at home with their parents. None was married, nor planned to be. They seemed like overage teenagers.

The word "teenager" appeared in American English in the 1940s to describe people who were no longer children but not yet adults. For decades it described a passing phase before people made commitments to marriage and career. Today in Western countries people still grow old, but many refuse to grow up. Others have noticed the phenomenon, for example, Diana West in her book *The Death of the Grown-up*.

People of earlier times saw life differently. Concepts like "senate" (Latin *senex* "old") "aldermen" ("elder" men), and "mayors" ("oldest") remind us that in other eras maturity and old age were regarded as the pinnacle of power and respect.

An invisible pendulum seems to swing between periods of youthful and elderly predominance. In earlier ages, if there was any happiness to be found in this world, it was in the wise counsel of the elderly; today the ideal seems to be the foolishness of youth.

What happens when the pendulum swings to youth? Consider these features: physical exuberance, sports, speed, bodily gratification, sentimental dullness, deteriorated language, and youthful forms of intelligence defined by an indifference to history, science, and tradition. On the upside, however, these youth-centered eras are marked by vast creative energy.

On the other hand, when the mature mindset predominates, tradition tends to smother creativity. These are the ages of power and protocol, religion and philosophy, order and empire, and, on the downside, institutionalized privilege and class inequalities.

We are not talking primarily of chronological age. In nearly all eras, leadership and power gravitate to individuals between the ages of forty-five and sixty-five. The question is whether their leadership has a youthful or mature cast. The great majority of the warriors and knights of the medieval chronicles and Crusades were impulsive youths. Romeo and Juliet were teenagers. It is said that all great Romantics died young, but they were precociously mature and melancholy in thought. On the other hand, Thomas Jefferson was a mature thirty-two or so when he wrote the Declaration of Independence.

Youth should be youthful, and the old, elderly without apology. After all, there is no alternative to being who we are at every stage of life. The falsification begins when the young try to be mature before their time and the elderly who want to stay young after youth has passed. The elderly are unable to do many youthful things, but the compensation is that they understand better the meaning of what they can still do.

Article 24: Boredom

Boredom is like ugly weeds that sprout in a manicured garden. After WWII supposedly assured peace for all time to come, social planners predicted a golden age of health, peace, prosperity, and amusements in which boredom would be unthinkable. The word itself was barely known. It first appeared in *Bleak House* (1852), one of Charles Dickens' lesser known novels. In earlier centuries the struggle for life was too demanding in Europe and America for boredom. Hungry people are not bored but desperate.

Yet despite these rosy predictions, boredom has become a generalized problem, perplexing in children, often dangerous in adolescents and young adults. I suspect that perhaps half of the public crimes committed today are not responses to actual hunger or want but dangerous ways to combat boredom.

Most people have never had more resources at their fingertips—games, sports, entertainment, books, movies, food, transportation, communications, etc. The problem, particularly with the young, is they have no plans or projects in which to put these things to use. Perhaps the most frequent complaint we hear from children and young people, is a plaintive "I'm bored."

Older generations often react to these complaints with indignation, reminding the young that in the old days they had far less. The scolding has a two-fold purpose: (1) to jolt the young out of their listlessness and (2) to remind them how wimpy they are in comparison to their tougher elders. It does not help at all, and usually makes things worse. And no wonder; to their boredom, which is real, their elders add humiliation, which the young naturally resent.

Few people can be expected to escape the modern curse of boredom by living the life of the mind, as Plato recommended in ancient times. But they can blow their minds away with stupefying drugs.

Well-meaning parents, counselors, and teachers usually tell young people that in addition to being illegal, drugs and alcohol are dangerous, even lethal. It is probably the worst message for youth to hear. They already know how dangerous these substances are. It is why they take them in the first place and why people risk their life attempting daredevil stunts: racing trains to the crossing, engaging in dangerous sex, committing crime, shooting drugs, and bingeing out with alcohol. Taking risks and challenging death are the ultimate human thrills. The problem is that death often wins.

If boredom is a root cause of these dangerous activities, what is the solution? I have no ready answer, only an observation. Like everybody else, young people want to be useful and respected. In times of crisis, most dangerous activities quickly disappear and unselfish heroism replaces them. It seems that only a commitment to a greater cause can get individuals out of their boredom and into their real selves. Easy to say, hard to do.

Article 25: Brotherhood of the Truthful

They were men and women who wrote in many languages and lived in different eras. Most were unacquainted with one another. Diverse in talents and outlooks, they were poets, scientists, philosophers, and mystics. Yet despite differences of language and style, we sense in them a closeness and a kinship that transcend time and culture. I call them a "brotherhood of the truthful." They approached the world with eager curiosity and the courage to accept it on its own terms without imposing prior conditions. Above all, they delighted in truth and were unafraid of its consequences.

Not that they appreciated the same things. As someone has said, every genuine personal perspective is a fraction of the cosmic whole. What Shakespeare or Milton offers us cannot be an accusation against Dante, Montaigne, Racine, Goethe, or Calderon, who had other visions, other nuggets of truth, to offer us. Probably no one has spoken more nobly than Jorge Manrique about the meaning of life and death. And who could fail to be inspired by the divine insights of Hildegard von Bingen? Nor must we think that truth is confined to fact. The truth of art, the beauty of music, need make no apologies to scientific theories. Nor vice versa. Newton, Leibnitz, and Descartes have a vision of truth that complements the best of dramatists and poets.

This brotherhood of the truthful possesses a vitality that protects its members against oblivion. And if we examine the reasons for their staying power, we discover a paradox. The popular themes of conventional writers and thinkers often are the same ones that explain their early disappearance. History shows that the more a writer or thinker succumbs to the biases and prejudices of the moment, the briefer the effective life of the work may be. Only the deeper, unbiased truths survive. The work of Herodotus, the first Western historian, is, despite its flaws, still treasured today, whereas countless histories have disappeared with scarcely a trace. In part, his fame is due to his historical priority, but the greater reason for his enduring appeal is his unbiased openness to the world, and perhaps even more, the delight he takes in preserving things worthy of remembrance.

The deep truths are timeless and equally timely. Plato and Aristotle are still very much with us, unlike other thinkers of much more recent vintage. Here let me add another reason for their longevity: their willingness to wrestle with the deepest questions of human life and fate: metaphysics, the mystery of human reality, ethics, ideal governance, and other matters that modern thinkers like to avoid. The Greek thinkers were often wrong, but they were uncommonly courageous. Instead of trusting in oracles and omens, as humanity had always done, they taught us to test our intellectual wings and soar on our own. This combination of sincerity, courage, and daring has characterized the "Brotherhood of the Truthful" ever since.

Article 26:
Cabeza de Vaca: The Second Saga

Most of us learned in history classes that the strange man known by the even stranger name of Cabeza de Vaca (Cow's Head, in reality an inherited honorific) was the first European in Texas, just as his companion, Estebanico, was the first African in what is now Texas. But perhaps fewer are aware of two other facts about Cabeza de Vaca. First, he is recognized as the first Texas surgeon. His name and family symbol appear on the Texas Surgical Society insignia. He was credited with near miraculous surgeries and healings, performed under the most primitive conditions, but he never claimed to be a medical doctor. Instead, he was a well-educated man who wrote a remarkable *Relación* (account) of his adventures. Unlike the mounted *conquistadores*, Cabeza de Vaca was never a conqueror, as the Spanish word implies, but at times enslaved, beaten, and nearly always afoot.

The second fact, which I call his "second saga," refers to exploits in South America almost as remarkable as his travels and travails in North America. Cabeza de Vaca was a man of great faith and remarkable endurance. Perhaps his main flaw was that he was too ambitious for his own good. Upon his return to Spain in 1537, where his patient wife María Marmelejo had awaited him for ten years, he pestered the Spanish court to give him a high-level appointment. Finally, in 1540, Emperor Charles V granted him a contract and named him military commander of Spanish forces in the Buenos Aires-Asunción region of South America. He organized a force of 250 men (26 mounted) and several wives, and in 1541 began the 1,200-mile trek to Asunción on the Paraguay River. The forest was almost impenetrable, but under his able leadership he lost only two men on the march: one to a jaguar, the other to an illness helped along by a wound. Equally remarkable, not a single horse was lost. In characteristic fashion, Cabeza de Vaca showed his solidarity by walking barefoot the entire distance. On the way, he and his group were the first Europeans to see the magnificent Iguazú Falls in 1542.

The beleaguered Spanish garrison greeted the relief force with cheers of joy. But the Spaniards soon turned against him when he tried to enforce decrees by the Spanish crown calling for humane treatment of native peoples. At many outposts in the far-flung Spanish empire the philosophy of local officials can be summed up in the expression, "I obey but I do not comply." Meanwhile, Cabeza de Vaca directed exploration of the Paraguay River wilderness hundreds of miles upstream.

Arrested, twice poisoned (but cured himself), and sent in chains to Spain, Cabeza de Vaca was declared guilty of ordering the inhumane treatment of native peoples, the very opposite of what he tried to do. Eventually pardoned, he died in 1559, having spent his remaining years writing the celebrated account of his adventures in both Americas.

Article 27: Cervantes and Don Quixote

Miguel de Cervantes was born in 1547 and died four centuries ago in 1616, the same day as Shakespeare. Both men are acknowledged as the peerless masters of their respective languages. If English is often called the "the language of Shakespeare," Spanish is commonly described as "the language of Cervantes." They share another oddity: a continuing controversy over who really wrote their masterpieces. Neither seemed to be a towering genius; their education was limited and their peers more impressive. Lope de Vega was the literary giant of Spain at the time. His fame was so great that anything of quality was said to be "of Lope."

Cervantes divided his life between military service and literature. He spent many years away from Spain and always considered the crowning achievement of his life to be the Battle of Lepanto (1571) in which the combined Christian fleets defeated the powerful Ottoman navy and checked the Islamic advance in Europe. Cervantes lost the use of his left arm in the battle and afterwards was known as the "cripple of Lepanto."

On the way home, he and his brother Rodrigo were captured and enslaved in Algeria for five years. Ransomed and back in Spain, he was a forgotten man, living precariously short of money and jailed for irregularities in some of his accounts. Scholars believe that during his jail sentence in Seville he began to write the first part of *Don Quixote,* destined to become the world's greatest novel.

Already old by the standards of his day, Cervantes could not compete on equal terms with Lope de Vega and other Spanish masters. Circumstances forced him to surpass them. The result was the story of Don Quixote and Sancho Panza, literature's best-known characters.

If most literature is taken from life, *Don Quixote* is life taken from literature. His neighbors gossiped that Don Quixote lost his mind from reading too many novels of chivalry. But Don Quixote himself believed his readings revealed to him who he was really meant to be. And the scoffers and mockers could not turn him from his conviction. Later, old and defeated in battle but undaunted in spirit, he would say proudly: "I know who I am." And to this he added: "The enchanters may take away fame and fortune, but not my effort and my striving."

Four ideals drive Don Quixote: freedom, valor, beauty, and love. He is the champion of freedom, the defining human quality often denied but never destroyed. Bruised and beaten, he never wavers in valor, nor does his vision of Lady Dulcinea weaken. Though not physically real, she is the deathless dream of beauty and love that drives him on his quest. Today we acknowledge him as the greatest knight errant of them all, the human symbol of all that is noble, lovely, and true, just as Sancho stands for abiding friendship, loyalty, and practicality. Together they strike a compelling human balance between idealism and realism.

Article 28: Chewing the Fat

Naval terminology is a part of mainstream English. "Chewing the fat" is an example. Today it means idle conversation, but once it referred to chewing on the leathery cured beef served to British or American sailors. Chewing on it, as people chew gum today, would soften it enough to swallow.

Ropes held heavy cannons securely in place on battleships, but occasionally one would break its moorings and roll uncontrollably as a "loose cannon," doing catastrophic damage to ship and crew. "Three sheets to the wind" referred to sails flapping uselessly in the wind, perhaps the work of sailors "groggy" from drinking too much grog. A "clean bill of health" was a document issued by a shipmaster attesting to the wellness of those on board. "Letting the cat out of the bag" referred to the cat-o-nine tails, or whip, used to flog lax or insubordinate sailors. The "cat" was kept in a baize bag when not in use. Today "hand over fist" describes rapid, efficient movement, but originally it described the agility of sailors climbing the shrouds, or nautical ropes, up to the mast of sailing ships. An expert sailor was one who "knew the ropes," or rigging. "Leeway" originally meant the navigable space between the ship and the leeward side, or shoreline. The "doldrums," which today indicates listlessness, once referred to oceanic regions near the equator where sailing ships were often becalmed in breezeless waters. "Taking the wind out of his sails" was a maneuver whereby a ship would sail to the windward side of an enemy vessel and block the wind. This caused its sails to droop, rendering it vulnerable to attack.

"Wallop" comes from the name of Admiral Wallop. After the French burned the English town of Brighton, King Henry VIII ordered him to retaliate. The admiral so "walloped" the French coast that his name became a fixture in English.

Sailors gathered around the "scuttlebutt," or water keg, as people still do, to relax and exchange gossip—or maybe to start it. We like for people to be "above board" in their dealings. It originally meant to be visible on deck with nothing to hide. However, not everything "above board" was what it seemed to be. Pirates would sometimes masquerade on deck as honest merchants, but their henchmen would be concealed on lower decks ready to attack and plunder the gullible.

Army and navy terminologies have different origins. Military terms in British and American armies are usually anglicized French words—bivouac, brigade, platoon, siege, cadre, sergeant, lieutenant, colonel. For centuries French armies set the military standard in Europe, but France was never a dominant naval power. This is why British and American navies use native English words, or borrow them from the Dutch. The "boom" in the expression "to lower the boom" on someone comes from the Dutch word *Bommen*. But if the boom, or spar, wallops you, it hurts the same in both languages.

Article 29: Some Thoughts about Cities

Did you hear that fifty-five percent of Parisians would prefer to live somewhere else? Are they kidding us? Is this the same Paris where tourists pay good money to be insulted, the capital of the Muslim world, the city that developed rudeness into an art form, the place where everybody woke up on the wrong side of the bed one day and stayed that way forever?

I couldn't tell you if there's any real French culture left in Paris. Some say it was lost in the generation of Hemingway, Stein, and Picasso. But at least it's still the best place in the world to study the ecological impact of six million dogs, imitation American fast food, and cars so ugly you wouldn't wish one on your ex-mother-in-law. In Gene Kelley's day everybody loved Paris in the springtime, rainy or not, but now it seems you can't keep them in Paree after they've seen the farm.

But let's be fair. It's not right to pile on old Paris. Less glamorous cities from Baltimore to Buffalo are not all that different. So tell me this: if nobody wants to live in them, how come urban sprawl is like the Blob that ate Cleveland? Hey, keep the cheering down. We'll have no applause for the Blob. And I hope what I see down the street is not people petitioning to offer it LA, Philadelphia, Memphis, and Detroit. Be nice and don't insult the Blob. It has its standards, too, you know.

So here's the deal: everybody speaks ill of the cities, but everybody lives in them. Last time I heard there were only a few farmers left in Iowa or some state up there still holding out, still growing food, of all things, for us professors, lawyers, CEOs, accountants, politicians, and other non-laboring types.

But let me make two points. First, gloomy thinkers warn us all the time about the coming collapse of Western civilization. Well, they shouldn't worry so much. It's already happened. Houston got rid of all that civilization stuff back around 1965 and does just fine without it. The other mistake they make is thinking the cities are swallowing up the countryside. I did some deep thinking on the matter—five or ten minutes at least—and decided it's really the other way around. So-called "urban sprawl" is really "urban dismemberment." We country people came to the city, demolished it, and then scattered the pieces all over the countryside.

I know. I know. You're going to tell me about all those tall buildings along any big city skyline, but you're just blowing smoke. They may look like a city, but it's only a mirage, because nobody but bums and a few artsy folks really live down there. Come five p.m., the wagon trains head out for the boonies and the place is empty. At night you wouldn't want to be caught dead downtown. Let me correct the redundancy: if you do get caught down there after dark, you're dead.

Article 30: Chicken Little

You know the story: an acorn falls and bounces off Chicken Little's head. She panics and runs away screaming that the sky is falling. Today it seems that Chicken Littles are everywhere and all are warning us that the sky is falling and assorted dooms are about to do us in.

Financial gurus warn us that our fiscal system is about to collapse. It is a selling tactic of investment experts to predict either boom or bust. If bust, then half the population will dismiss them as dolts, but if boom, the other half will hail them as geniuses and climb aboard their investment bandwagon. Money matters even as the world lurches to an end.

Medical scientists warn us that "superbugs" immune to all known antibiotics could—and may—kick off world-wide epidemics. On the other side of the lethal ledger, overpopulation, dwindling food supplies, and lack of water may lead to the mass extinction of human and animal populations. The Y2K concern, the Mayan Calendar excitement of 2012, and similar predictions verify human obsession with the end of the world.

Then there are the classic threats of nuclear destruction. I recall walking along State Street in Chicago many years ago, thinking that today the Russians may drop the Bomb on us and there's no place to hide. Meanwhile, hundreds of thousands of school children were crouching under their desks in public schools while their parents were building bomb shelters in their back yards. We have forgotten that those good old days offered a daily dose of terror.

As if these dangers were not bad enough, I heard recently that the honeybees that pollinate our plants are dying and that soon we shall have no food as a result. Just days ago I read that careening around the Solar System are hundreds of objects big enough to devastate our world. It's only a matter of time until one does. Oh, and did I mention that our coastal cities are sinking? Meanwhile, Hollywood floods the screen and our minds with space aliens and apocalyptic zombies that may wipe us out. And if all other catastrophes fail, astronomers tell us that eventually the sun will expand and cook the earth to a cinder.

Chicken Littles tell us daily that new chunks of the sky are falling. But so far their prophetic record is dismal. Acorns still fall but the world yet abides. Manmade or natural calamities do happen and sensible people know we have a responsibility to care for the earth. But philosopher David Hume cautioned against assuming effects when we are ignorant of certain causes. Chance is one, Emerson's deep remedial force is another. They work together to reshape the old and outworn things of earth. Destruction is a dimension of renewal. The process has kept the world in business for a long time, and despite our Chicken Littles, I would not be surprised if it continues a good while longer.

Article 31:
Seasonal Code Words

Certain words, like certain colors, are seasonally coded, and none more so than our Christmas vocabulary. With Thanksgiving now behind us and Christmas just ahead, the yearly ritual of Christmas trees, bright lights, ornaments, cards, and gifts gets into full swing. And with them music and expressions we hear at no other time of the year. For several days Bing Crosby, Dean Martin, Nat King Cole, Burl Ives, Gene Autry, and other singers from generations long gone return for yet another encore. It is unrealistic to dream of a white Christmas in semi-tropical Houston, but the non-stop Christmas music of yesteryear reminds us anyway of snowy images nearly everywhere we go.

Then December 26th dawns and suddenly it is all over except bargain shopping, returns, and the work of taking it all down. We discover that unlike the winter Texans who come south to escape the cold, Santa Claus has jingled his way back to the farthest north, taking the Christmas magic with him. Rap and rock replace the old songs and songsters until next year, and as we pack away the ornaments we also put away certain words that we hardly ever say in other seasons.

For example, we seldom hear the word "merry" outside the Christmas context or in the Christmas carol about "merry gentlemen." We could, but likely would not, wish someone a "merry birthday" or a "pleasant Christmas," though lately I notice that "happy holidays" is gaining traction. True, some people still say "making merry" or "having a merry old time," but these expressions sound a bit stilted and are generally limited to the older generation. Much the same can be said of hymns about the Nativity. "Silent Night" or "O Little Town of Bethlehem" would seem as misplaced in a Texas summer as Wassail at a Fourth of July celebration.

For reasons only indirectly associated with Christmas itself, to wish someone a "merry Christmas" has become the focus of a bitter controversy in recent times. Christmas itself has long had a bit of schizophrenia about it. Is it a holiday or a holy day? Is it basically a Nordic winter festival or a Christian holy event? Obviously it is both in varying degrees. But despite efforts to reconcile the differences, the focus was never quite settled internally even before it mutated in recent years into a contentious clash between secularist and religious points of view.

Unlike Fourth of July events, Christmas has never been a patriotic holiday. It was ancient long before the Spanish and English brought earlier versions of it to North America. On the other hand, Thanksgiving, the most iconic American holiday, has both religious and nationalistic overtones. As far as I know, Uncle Sam never appears in the company of Santa Claus, or the Pilgrim Fathers, and much less the Easter Bunny. All these holidays/holy days and their assorted symbolisms are associated with different terminology, music, sentiments, and forms of celebration.

Article 32: Colliding Theories

Today there are two colliding theories of human life with many religious and scientific subsets. Consider, if you will, a summary of another variation on this ancient theme.

If we view the human creature scientifically as an anthropoid animal, then it is logical to conclude that humans are duplicate, replaceable specimens, like cattle in a herd or bees in a hive. Given this paradigm, claims of transcendent significance for individual beings may be dismissed as delusional fictions, as indeed, they usually are.

But as a being that foresees life and ponders its meaning, a person is a "finite infinitude," as one philosopher puts it. In the first theory, the human organism ends in biological death; yet from an internal perspective, we find not theoretical boundaries to personhood, but discover our life to be a projective, futuristic creation of dreams and designs. To be a person is to be always capable of becoming more so. Unlike the limited "real" world of things and animals, human reality includes as its greater portion unlimited, unrealized potentialities.

A person is never given once and for all, but instead is always coming into being. Personal life is dramatic, expectant, and pregnant with future possibilities. As persons, we must imagine our life before we can live it. Without this foresight in ourselves and others—including fictional persons—literature and the arts would be as impossible for us as they are meaningless to animals. Taxonomy is sufficient to describe an animal, but we cannot understand people without knowing their times, ambitions, events, and story of their life, in short, their biography. A new-born animal is in miniature what it will be forever. But a person is always emerging into the life, always being born, always composing a narrative, sometimes a symphony.

The prime task of personal life is, naturally, to personalize the world, conforming it to our narrative and striving for a personal accommodation with its obstacles and resources. Unlike animals, we cannot depend on instincts, for ours are vestigial remnants, like snake legs or bird teeth. Instead, personal being consists in the necessary freedom to reason, justify, and rectify. In nature most animals are rank cowards, living in a state of instinctual alertness ever ready to volatilize into terrorized flight. Humans may also lapse into animal panic, for without instincts everything personal must be learned, and we have not mastered all our lessons. Personal life also consists of alertness, but it is intellectual, not instinctual, and definable as the power to reason in moments of fear and peril. We call it courage.

But life must confront finalities. In the first theory, death seems biologically simple. Yet when examined internally, personal reality is neither simple nor simply biological. The premise of personal life as an ever-emerging reality raises suspicions that a logical fallacy occurs when we switch from personal to biological categories in order to declare an end to creative personhood that by definition and process is endless.

Article 33: Condition or Situation?

We use the terms "condition" and "situation" interchangeably to describe our moods and status, but when we speak of the "human condition" we mean our unchangeable way of being in the world, as men or women, for example, or as mortals who must die someday. "Certain death at an uncertain hour," the ancient Romans put it.

"Situation" is primarily location, but it also has wider meanings: states of illness, wellbeing, hunger, fear, or anger. If I say I am a man, it implies my human condition, but if I tell you that I am stranded at an airport, I am describing my situation.

Both our condition and situation have forms of happiness and unhappiness attached to them, but commonly we associate them with our situation. If I am employed—a situation—then I am reasonably content, but if unemployed, worried and unhappy.

Unhappiness with one's condition is rare but more drastic. In former times, to be unhappy with one's gender, for instance, was irremediable. A man who felt he should be a woman, or a woman who wanted to be a man, were tragic figures without hope of changing their condition.

Today we see that conditions once considered unchangeable are becoming situational. Upward mobility in America broke the first age-old conditional barriers, and others continue to fall. Now it is possible, legally at least, for a man to become a woman, and a woman, a man. The same is true of divorce. Instead of the lifetime condition it once was—"till death do us part"—marriage is becoming a situational matter subject to change.

The trend away from fixed conditions to transitional situations not only creates controversy but also injects a note of disorientation into society. But with a curious twist: in former times, the young were more likely to be unsure of their place in the world; today it is adults and the elderly who are perplexed. Not that all conditions have turned situational. Despite greater longevity, age and death remain part of the human condition. We still get old and we still die.

All these changes devolve on a single impulse: the urge for happiness, the foundation of our human condition. The matters that fill our life—our faith, education, vocation, the belongings we accumulate, the schemes we hatch, and, especially, the persons we love—are intended to make us happy. Fulfillment is our aim and it is one with happiness. Pleasures are plural and passing, but happiness, which curiously has no plural form, stakes a limitless claim to our future. It is what we can embrace forever.

Yet because we are futuristically oriented beings with unfinished lives, we are never fully happy in this life. We pursue happiness and for that very reason are more familiar with its deficient twin we call unhappiness. We cannot capture happiness once and for all, but neither can we live without its image and the hope of achieving it. For this reason, happiness has been called "the necessary impossibility."

Article 34: Contagious!

Probably we are all contagious to some degree. No, hopefully not with viral or bacterial illnesses but with attitudes and behaviors. For example, you may have noticed that if a driver zips by you on the freeway at nearly the speed of sound, other drivers speed up in response. Soon a caravan of macho drivers zooms ahead in competitive fury, leaving us feeling either a bit sheepish for our timidity, or hoping that the police will pull them over as we drive smugly by.

Dour, surly people without a kind word cast a pall over everybody around them, and we hurry to get away from them. But those who are pleasant and friendly attract us to their convivial company. The old saying that it takes more muscles to frown than to smile may be true or not—I confess I don't know—but a smile brightens the scene and leaves a residual glow of good feeling.

Usually we respond positively to enthusiastic people, unless they cross an invisible line and bore us with a cause that has become an obsession. Few people are a greater turnoff than the person on a soapbox.

Body language speaks volumes. The droopy, hangdog look and downcast eyes of certain people can drain us of energy, but so can those who do all they can to keep our attention when our eyes have glazed over and we are screaming inwardly to escape.

My recipe for escaping moments of funk is to whisper a silent prayer for people who annoy me, grab the only parking spot, or take the better part of an hour to check out at the grocery or post office. On my better days I say the prayers randomly for strangers I pass on the street or the road. Why? I can't say for sure. I just feel more contagious on those days. Besides, the philosopher Emerson said that we all lead lives of quiet desperation, which means we all need help.

There are people, like wells that never run dry, who possess magnanimously contagious spirits: great coaches, leaders, and motivators. I like to be in their company just in case a little of their magic rubs off on me. And I find that dressing the part of a happy, contagious person is a step toward being one. Conversely, if I dress sloppily, it surprises me how quickly I live down to the image. We have decided collectively that how we dress has nothing to do with who we are. "Come just as you are," we tell everybody. It may be a mistake, for it leads them to expect no big deal and that they can go home just as they were. Maybe we should be telling them, "Come better than you are," for acting better than we are is a big step to becoming better than we have been. And it is contagious.

Article 35:
Dressed for the Occasion

Sometimes it's okay to be a man. Just think, no fashion worries of any kind, no makeup or jewelry, no thought to warts or wrinkles, untrimmed beards or nail polish. And no hard decisions about shoes: we wear the same pair everywhere. Combinations and seasonal colors are no problem. Whatever comes up next in the clothes closet is fine. And if a brown sock is missing, a blue one will do nicely. Scuffy or stuffy, rude or crude, our choices are easy.

My old stomping ground, the academic world, is tailored for men. There, shabbiness is always stylish. Professors insinuate by example that an untidy appearance is a sign of an original mind. The students eat it up, which sometimes makes it hard to tell a university class from a huddle of homeless people. But the world being the unfair place that it is, women professors do not fare as well. Students think shabbiness is cool in male professors, but in women, well, not so cool, in fact just plain shabby.

In the real world, men never notice or care what other men wear, and if women are shocked by how a man dresses, they usually make comments only to other women. If the man is married, instead of criticizing him—innocent creature that he is—they blame the wife for letting her largest domestic pet roam around town dressed like a street person.

And things only get better as a man gets older. No matter how outlandishly an old man dresses, folks either assume his clothes are fashions from his prehistoric past or think that in his diminished mental state he is no longer responsible for his trespasses against good taste. In either case, people are okay with it. Old men get away with a lot.

But there are also thorns in this bed of roses. Life for men is one big imbalance. By the time most reach emotional and intellectual maturity—if ever—they are already in physical decline. So no sooner do they figure out what's going on than they are too decrepit to do much about it.

In most families, concerned, intelligent women look after men and try to see that they are dressed for the occasion. Men listen but do not hear them. It is my professional opinion that men suffer from a deadly deafness to the female voice. Science needs to investigate.

This odd male deafness may cause cosmic ripples. At her beloved's funeral the wife orders him laid out in a proper suit and tie—as usual, he's not listening. He religiously avoided such attire all his life, like the front pew at church, but now may have to wear it forever. Poetic justice perhaps?

Article 36: Drinking in Old Texas

German traveler Ferdinand Roemer observed during the era of the Texas Republic that "Texians, being entirely a military people, not only fought but drank in platoons." And a British visitor of that period, Francis Sheridan, remarked: "The passion for erecting grog shops supersedes the thirst of religious worship and Temples wherein to exercise it, for though we find every town plentifully supplied with Pot-Houses [taverns], we see neither a church nor signs of building one."

Corn mash whiskey, or Bourbon, after Bourbon County, Kentucky, was the common drink. Early Texans were not beer drinkers. Beer was considered too bland for serious drinkers and too strong for people who simply wanted a thirst quencher. It was only after German immigrants introduced "lager" brewing that beer caught on. However, Texans did drink persimmon beer, and in the larger cities such as Houston and Galveston imported cognac, champagne, brandy, gin, rum, and various wines could be had. However, wine was not a common beverage even though grapes were plentiful.

Most early Texans were descended from hard-drinking Anglo-Saxons and were in no way inferior to them in their drinking habits. Life was hard and drinking was one of the few pleasures available to them. Besides, they believed that alcohol had medicinal virtues and could cure old infections and prevent new ones. Another argument was that the water was bad in many towns. Restraint was for most an unknown discipline. Sipping their liquor might be fine for gentlemen of leisure, but in the disapproving words of visitor John Hunter Herndon in 1837, "It appeared to be the business of the great mass of the people to collect around these centers of vice and hold their drunken orgies..."

Drinking had its etiquette. First of all, it was considered a violation of drinking protocol not to invite all within a reasonable distance to join in. Second, drinking was done standing so as not to take up too much time. This permitted the process to be repeated four or five times a day.

Women drank, though usually not so copiously as men and with greater discretion. It was a general breach of social decorum for women to enter a tavern or hotel bar room.

As one would expect, drunkenness and alcoholism were problems. A newspaper editorial noted that "... the graveyard held scores of young men who died from intemperance." The problem was not confined to Texas. Historian Gerald Carson called this period "... the dark age of American drinking." Nevertheless, the temperance movement did not become a social and political force until the decades following the Civil War. It took years for most Texas towns to have as many churches as saloons and before Texans came to disapprove of excessive drinking. In the days of the Republic a "teetotaler" (meaning one who had taken a pledge of "total" abstinence) would have been scorned for failing to meet what were considered in those times the standards of common manhood.

Article 37:
Early Texas Education

"School days, school days, /Dear old Golden Rule days/ Readin' and 'ritin' and 'rithmetic/ Taught to the tune of a hick'ry stick." Though mushy with nostalgia, these 1907 lyrics by Will Cobb and Gus Edwards tell a great deal of truth about elementary education not only in the Texas Republic but throughout the United States in the 1840s.

Education was earnest in purpose but haphazard in organization. The image of the quaint little red schoolhouse belongs to a later time. In the early days, schools were housed in log cabins, churches, or abandoned structures. One old former teacher recalled that on winter mornings she and the bigger boys had to drive the goats from her dilapidated classroom, clean the floors, and build a fire in the wood heater before beginning recitations.

There was little separation by age. Children of all ages recited their lessons together. Students memorized selections from readers, competed in spelling bees, and called out geographies aloud. They were not allowed to question, criticize or interpret what they had memorized. If they did, corporal punishment might be the result, the size of the switch matching the size of the boy. However, corporal punishment was rarely applied to girls. Obedience, morality, and patriotic values were emphasized, not intellectual development. It was probably a good thing, for many teachers were only marginally educated themselves.

Throughout the nineteenth century, Noah Webster's *Spelling Book*, called the "Blue Back Speller," was a standard text on correct spelling and other features of the English language. Other textbooks were the *McGuffey Eclectic Readers* series, the *Hieroglyphical Bible,* and the vast selection of readers written or edited by Samuel Goodrich under the pseudonym of Peter Parley. All these books portrayed a world in which virtue was rewarded and vice punished. The Parley readers, in particular, extolled the American ideal and gave the general impression that it was superior to all others.

Women were encouraged to get an education, but the ulterior motive was so they could teach their own children if schools were not available. Consequently, by 1850 it is estimated that over 88% of white men and almost 80% of white women were literate. Blacks had little access to educational opportunities. Yet a good many Blacks became literate, sometimes with the help of sympathetic whites, in others, by their own determined efforts.

Despite a constitutional mandate that a general system of education be enacted, Texas trailed other states. While many states were passing child labor laws and truancy legislation, rural Texas continued to view children as a source of farm labor. Basic education was valued, but it was limited to a bare knowledge of "readin', 'ritin' and 'rithmetic," as the old lyrics describe. Not until 1915 was compulsory education enacted into law in Texas. And the "hick'ry stick" stuck around many years after that.

Article 38: Preferring the Preferable

The roots of language we call etymology often conceal fundamental truths. Take the word 'elegant', which derives from the ancient Latin verb *elegir*, or *eleguir* in its oldest form, meaning to choose, elect or select. In several modern European languages, including English, it has become a general synonym for things we consider to be elite, among them admirable lifestyles, tasteful acquisitions, and graceful behavior. It is the opposite of tacky decisions and clumsy conduct.

Elegance may characterize our selection of cars and clothing, but its basic meaning goes much deeper to the selections of which our life consists. There is no way around the process. To select is to exercise the unavoidable freedom of human life. And therein lies the paradoxical rub. We are condemned to freedom, as a couple of the modern philosophers put it. This means that the most fundamental freedom denied us is the freedom not to be free. We may choose to let others decide for us, but that in itself is an act of freedom. The imperative of deciding is a peculiarly human burden.

Our life choices are not all equally valid or enticing, but appear to us as hierarchies and levels with value labels attached to them. This imposes on us the responsibility of justifying our preferences. Otherwise, all our choices would be as simple as picking a card at random. Here intelligence, another member of the ancient elegance family comes into play. Intelligence comes from *int-elegir* and is also related to *legere*, to read, to discern, to be able to select wisely. All these words are related to elite, another member of this group. The truly elite and elegant among us are those who make intelligent decisions and judgments. To do otherwise is to commit a transgression, first against ourselves, or worse, a partial suicide, in which, as another philosopher put it, we are at once the author, victim, and judge of our errors. Inelegant choices diminish us. Other opportunities may come, but this squandered occasion will not. Linking all these words, we can say that intelligence allows us to make the elegant choices. The elegant person does not stumble or misjudge, but gets things right; the author who writes an imperishable work; the musician who plays with incomparable skill; the scientist who offers us new insights into the Cosmos.

All this points to deeper connections. The elegant life that consists of right choices and justifiable decisions hints that true intelligence must have an ethical dimension. Ethics and intelligence go together like a hand and a glove. Without an ethical foundation intelligence risks sinking to mere cleverness, the inelegant, willing servant of demagogues and deceivers whose main business has always been the destruction of civilizations.

We admire elegance because it readily divides humanity into two classes: those who simply cannot see its connections to anything else beyond momentary convenience and others who see in it the fine art of preferring the preferable.

Article 39: Europe's Inverted Pyramid

Outwardly nothing seems different in Europe. It still has its historic cities, great art, superb food, and quaint byways where old centuries still linger. None of that has changed, and in fact, as I noticed on my recent trips there, much has gotten better. The marriage of American ingenuity and continental finesse allows Europe to remain the center of world tourism without the antiquated technology that once bedeviled travelers to the Old World.

But the most basic resource is missing. Europeans have no children. I overstate the fact to make the point, but there is no disputing the demographics. Birthrates in France, Italy, Spain, Greece, and Northern Europe have fallen below replacement levels. Only Russia has managed to pull slightly ahead of the death curve for the first time in decades.

The rest of Europe is fast becoming an inverted pyramid with an aging population as the broad top tier and a shrunken replacement generation at the upside-down apex unable to fund the pensions and medical needs of elderly retirees.

For several decades in post-WWII Europe, schools, parks, and playgrounds were full of children. It took a whole generation for European women to get used to the Pill, which for the first time in history separated sex and reproduction. But by 1990 the demographic decline was noticeable. This was followed by legislative approval of divorce and then abortion. Birthrates plunged and have not yet bottomed out.

Today a large percentage of young Europeans choose the single, childless life. Sex is casual and non-committal. Even if they marry, many couples elect not to have children for economic reasons. Employment is precarious, and the centralized Euro, which seemed a fine idea when it was adopted, does not let individual countries control their monetary policies. Encouraged by the United States, Spain went heavily green. The ecological improvements were commendable but the economic results disastrous.

But does any of this really matter to Americans? Consider two reasons why it does. First, Europeans readily adopt American technology, educational theory, business models, fashion, and entertainment. Second, in slower, reverse cycles, America also follows European trends by repeating what Europe has done. The European nations went into socialist mode decades before issues such as socialized medicine, social justice, welfare, and centralization of power became political hot buttons in America.

The conclusion is axiomatic: if you want to know what America will be like in the future, look at what Europe is today.

This brings up European fears about the future. I said that the Europeans have no children. But other populations, particularly the Muslims, have plenty of children. The older Europeans I talked with are fearful that with its burgeoning Islamic population, France will reach a demographic tipping point in about twenty-five years and declare itself a Muslim nation. At the same time, however, most French people seem confident that in time younger Muslims will abandon Islam and become secularized French citizens. As for the Muslims, who do not consider themselves Europeans and show little interest in European democracy except as a pathway to power, their plan is simple: stay the Islamic course and breed their way to political and religious dominance. Today France and the rest of Europe are in a race against time to see which strategy wins out.

Article 40: Happiness or Exasperation?

Europeans used to call Americans "the happy people" and many still have the old American stereotype fixed in their mind. The Europeans find it strange that Americans ask family and friends to smile for photographs. Older Europeans and other nationalities consider smiling to be undignified for men and provocative in women. In the past—and still in some places—American women were pestered for smiling at Latin American, Middle Eastern, and southern European men. From their cultural perspective, a "no" said with a smile is really a coy "yes." Generally speaking, Europeans still expect Americans to have a smiling disposition and a good sense of humor. The "happy people" are still expected to be happy, and they do not know exactly what to make of Americans who do not play the part. The American stereotype is alive and well even if the reality is not.

Recently in Spain I was reminded of "happy America." Thirty high-school students had missed their flight and were stranded in my hotel. They looked American but seemed too polite and happy. I asked a waitress about them. She told me they spoke English, which she didn't, so they had to be either British or American. "Probably British," I told her, thinking that American students would be noisy and verbal about being inconvenienced. I was wrong; they were Americans, but perhaps not typical. They were from farms and ranches in Kansas and Nebraska, and this was the first time abroad not only for them but also for their teachers. They had made the mistakes that tourists make, but their spirits were undaunted. I congratulated them and their teachers on the fine way they represented our country, and did what I could to help them. We were on the same flight to Chicago. Old America still lives, I thought nine hours later as the plane touched down to their cheers and laughter.

O'Hare Airport was a jolting return to a different America. No smiles there, only rude, resentful employees. It was a stark reminder that the exasperation we witness in places like O'Hare is not isolated unpleasantness but erosion of the quality of American life.

Are we letting our problems become bigger than we are? I wondered. And who are we anyway? Persons with the inalienable birthright to pursue happiness. These happy students annoyed some people at O'Hare. Unhappily, many Americans have bought into the bogus doctrine that no one has a right to be happy as long as others are unhappy, that it is wrong to prosper until everyone prospers. But to me it is weird alchemy to think that we can dilute the world's supply of misery by adding ours to it.

Sometimes we have to relearn what we already know. The happy students I met in Spain reminded me of America's real heritage. Kansas and Nebraska, send us more like them!

Article 41: Facing up to Life

Life is a matter of facing the future, and our face records the experience. Behind our genetic and racial features, the vision of the future we pursue and what happens to us in the process show in our face. Our purpose or pretense, kindness or cruelty, success or failure, happiness or misery, all mark our facial features. Our face is a living etching of who we have been, tried to be, or failed to become. As Shakespeare says, "God has given you one face, and you have made yourselves another."

Love is life's most exhilarating experience. This is why true lovers never tire of staring at the beloved's face, especially the eyes. For despite Hollywood exaggerations, what real lovers do most is look and talk, both of which are facially concentrated. If a man pays more attention to a woman's anatomy than her face, he is acting out of lust, not love. This is why it generally annoys women when men who interest them stare at their body. They get the real message, and it is not love.

Because the face reflects human reality, we cannot say that a woman is beautiful or a man handsome without reference to their face. A torso is impersonal, somewhat like a mannequin, and an expressionless face on an otherwise ideal body disappoints our aesthetic expectations. The body is biologically erotic, but the face is humanly erogenous.

Most faces are not beautiful or handsome. A woman may choose not to beautify herself, but if so, she ignores her feminine condition. Not that she must be beautiful in order to be a woman, but womanhood requires that she try to be as attractive as she can be. In a parallel way, a man may not possess great physical strength, but he must try to be strong in order to be a man. Man is weak by nature but strong by necessity.

It comes as no surprise that women have fared better than men in modern feminist psychology. For decades man has been ridiculed as a pompous imposter, claiming to be strong when he is not. But it is important to distinguish between claiming to be strong and trying to be. The honest man knows that he does not possess all the strength, knowledge, and power he seeks—otherwise he would not seek them to start with. He claims these traits even though he does not fully possess them because they define what it means to be a man

Not that his case is unique. For both men and women living is trying to be who we have not yet become. This is why we must live from the future. It pulls us forward, as a locomotive pulls the train cars behind it. It is the only way out of our problems. Only in the future can we hope to resolve our dilemmas, correct our mistakes, and make a run for happiness.

Article 42:
Familiar Falsehoods

Humans are supposedly the smartest of species, but we commit and tolerate errors that in similar proportions probably would doom any other earthly species to extinction. Animals that teach their young to ignore predators or eat the wrong kind of food or birds that fail to build proper nests for their eggs and hatchlings would not last long. For animals there is only a right way and a wrong way; right means a chance to live but wrong is death. But we humans survive in complex combinations of the two. The fact that unlike other creatures, we can do so, is an astonishing reality but so obvious that philosophy and science generally have not even considered it. But leaving the topic for another day, consider two examples among many we could cite.

For generations we have accepted the opinion forcefully expressed by historian Thomas Carlyle that history does not reveal its alternatives, that it is a story already told and thus without suspense or interest, as many students believe. But at its core history is a drama of alternatives, the ultimate human novel. Human life consists primarily of making choices, individually and collectively, of choosing this life pathway or that, this way of life or another, this destiny or a tempting alternative, and of hitting the mark or going wide of the target in our choices. In each case we must justify, first to ourselves, our selection or rejection of alternatives. Even in the most desperate circumstances, as both Shakespeare and the existential philosophers point out, we still have the options of continuing in our wearying life or ending it by choice. In this most pathetic of decisions normally we think of individuals. But whole tribes and peoples have preferred death to an unacceptable fate. Think of the Jewish Masada or the Iberian Numantia.

Even more compatible with our contemporary thinking is the popular assertion that "violence is not the answer." And with it the still more dogmatic corollary: "Violence solves nothing." But we are apt to give these answers without first asking the questions. What problem are we talking about when we make these sweeping assertions? As far as I know, military violence was an effective solution to British colonial oppression, German Nazism, Japanese imperialism, and American slavery. None of which has resurfaced.

Nevertheless, these convictions have led to a belief that force itself, particularly military force, is inherently evil. War, which used to be "the solution to problems that have no solution," as a French minister once said, is now seen as a remedy worse than the disease. This has given rise to the favored alternative we call diplomacy. But diplomatic successes are scant and failures the norm. Historically, diplomacy was the polite face of military power. Today it has become little more than a currency exchange in which wealthy nations pay rogue regimes for promises of good behavior. But since misbehavior is more lucrative, the latter soon return to old patterns.

Article 43: Forbidden Questions

A century ago at the peak of the Modern Age, philosophers and scientists had reached general agreement that human destiny, Deity, and cosmic purpose with their heavy load of mystery and mysticism were forbidden questions. Because they could not be answered, they should not be asked.

An illustrious parade of agnostic or atheistic thinkers in science and philosophy—Bentham, Spencer, Comte, Schopenhauer, Pavlov, Russell, Sartre, Haldane, and many others—established or defended the Modern creed. It presents God not as the Creator of the Cosmos, but as a bothersome relic of a bygone, credulous age unnecessary in the modern paradigm of reality. And if unnecessary, then without valid arguments for his necessary existence.

The human corollary logically followed: if there was no divine guarantor of human fate, then mankind could make no valid claims to an afterlife. These and other likeminded thinkers shunted all such discussions off to theology, which they regarded as the dustbin of meaningless matters.

But the Modern Age has passed, and we are a hundred years into a new phase of history, as yet unnamed. And our views have likewise changed. What the Modern Age considered its highest virtue we are now beginning to see as its greatest failure. It consisted of two mistakes. First, the Moderns reasoned that if they could not answer the ultimate questions, then no one could. They believed themselves to be superior not only to all past eras but also to all future time. Their solution was to narrow the intellectual playing field and to define it by what it excluded rather by what it contain. And they expected future generations to obey the restrictions. Modernity was an archly imperialistic era in which each art, country and science sought to establish its dominance. The same imperialistic vision that inspired Cecil Rhodes to build countries inspired Richard Wagner to create heroic music.

The second error was even more serious. The Moderns failed to understand that it is not the answers that stimulate science and philosophy but the questions themselves. The first thinkers in ancient Greece asked the basic questions and at first came up with simplistic answers. For instance, they taught variously that combinations of fire, water, earth, and air were the basic components of all things. From our perspective, it is a laughable hypothesis. But if we stop there we misjudge the importance of their efforts. Instead of relying on omens and oracles, as they always had, for the first time these philosopher-scientists turned their intellect to the task of explaining the world. It was to be the pattern of progress from then on, not from the first answers, which often are wrong, but from persistently asking the right questions.

Today, we lack answers, but we have new perspectives and, most important, we have the questions. Now that the old restrictions of the Moderns no longer apply, hasn't the time has come to begin asking again the forbidden questions?

Article 44: Patriot or Traitor?

The South was anything but solid when it came to secession from the Union in 1861. The entire Appalachian mountain region from Virginia to North Alabama mainly opposed secession and sent many man to fight for the Union—among them my paternal Great-Grandfather. Pockets of resistance existed further west in Mississippi and Texas. The Virginia mountaineers even formed their own state that was admitted to the Union in 1863 as West Virginia.

In North Alabama fiery unionist orator and educator Charles Christopher Sheats (1839-1904) persuaded Winston County to declare itself Unionist and stand alone. It became known as "The Free State of Winston." For more than a hundred years after Reconstruction it sent the lone Republican representative to the Alabama state legislature. Alabama took revenge by neglecting its roads and infrastructure. But today the proud, independent Winston citizens are thankful for the neglect, for it left its forests, mountains, and wildlife in their pristine state and made it a mecca for nature lovers.

Home Guard units from Tuscaloosa County constantly harassed the Winston scalawags, as the Confederates derisively called them, killing some of them and forcing others to hide out in the Morgan County mountains. In 1863 Union Colonel Abel Strait led a force across the mountains to give relief to the loyalists. But at the Battle of Day's Gap wily Confederate General Nathan Bedford Forest outmaneuvered him, chasing the federal troops to exhaustion and surrender at Rome, Georgia.

Sheats won election to the Alabama legislature, but was expelled because he would not pledge allegiance to the Confederacy. Accused of "giving aid and comfort to the enemy and inducing citizens of this state to enlist as soldiers in the army of the United States," he was arrested, held without trial, and not finally released until 1865. He studied law and was admitted to the bar in 1867. In 1869 President Grant appointed him Consul at Elsinore, Denmark. In 1872 he was elected to one term in the U.S. House of Representatives, but lost his bid for reelection. Later he was appointed appraiser of merchandise for the Port of Mobile and served as assistant state collector of internal revenue. Afterwards, he held several minor positions and spent his final years managing his farm.

It is hard to separate truth from slander in his biography. Enemies accused Sheats of various misbehaviors, but it appears that most of these accusations arose from political animosity and not misdeeds. None could deny that he was fearless in defending what he believed was right. His portrait shows a handsome, well-featured face with a penetrating, intelligent look. In his own time he was both heartily despised as a traitor and cordially praised as a patriot. But his own epitaph, which I read recently on his tombstone in a rural Morgan County cemetery, probably gives the best assessment:

> I love my country, my God, and my kind.
> I have served them all.
> I want no praise of song or prose.

Article 45: Foretelling the Future

Nearly everybody wonders what the future holds, and some people spend time and money trying to find out in advance. But is there any sure way to know what tomorrow holds for us? Attempts to foretell the future are as old as humanity and nearly as common in our day as they were in ancient times. Celebrities, who tend to be superstitious, consult their gurus and fortunetellers. We may say publicly that enlightened people don't believe in such things, but how many of us sneak a look at our daily horoscope?

Since prehistoric times rulers and common people alike have heeded omens and oracles not only to learn their personal destiny but also to devise policies and fight wars. Threatened by Xerxes' huge Persian armada in 480 B.C., General Themistocles interpreted the Delphic oracle that Greece would be saved by "wooden walls" to mean that they must take to their ships. They did and routed the Persians in one of history's pivotal battles.

Prophetic predictions fall into three general categories with several subsets and overlaps: (1) the interpretation of sacred texts such as the Bible; (2) private revelations, for instance, the writings of Nostradamus; (3) and oracles, omens, tarot, tea leaves, séances, I Ching, hallucinogens, dreams, trances, and palmistry.

Unlike religious or private prophetic insights, a separate category of predictions consists of extrapolations of future events from observable scientific phenomena or historical trends.

Vague language characterizes many prophecies. In 480 B.C. many Greeks thought the cryptic Delphic statement that Greece would be saved by "wooden walls" meant that they should take refuge in the wooden Athenian Citadel. The Persian army slaughtered all who did. Nostradamus' statements have been teased and tortured to support many historical events. On the private level, experienced fortunetellers know that most people are interested in the same things: love, health, career, and the fate of loved ones. A single statement that happens to ring true in these areas will often offset any number of misses in others.

Still pending religious prophecies are customarily subject to a double set of interpretations: (1) the primary revelations such as those found in Revelation or the Book of Daniel, and (2) calculations about their timing. To most believers the overarching prophecies, often referred to as end-time events, are articles of faith. In Christianity, at least, the Scriptures warn against speculating when they will occur. This has not stopped imprudent minds from making countless false predictions.

The accuracy of scientific and historically-based predictions is almost as bad. A review of things predicted since WWII, for example, will show how inaccurate many of them were. And for a good reason: they failed to expect the unexpected.

But I ask again, can we foresee the future? There is too much evidence to deny the possibility, but too little to prove it. Tomorrow is another day, and perhaps we should let it tell its own story instead of trying to add its narrative to ours.

Article 46: Medicine in Frontier Texas

During the Texas Republic (1836-1846) the average life span was only about 39 years. High infant mortality was a key factor. Families had numerous children, but many died early. Many mothers also died in childbirth, partly because of a religious belief that anesthesia and other aids, even if available, should not be used since women were supposed to give birth "in sorrow."

Whiskey was a common painkiller during surgery, but many women refused it. In 1847, Sam Houston's wife Margaret was operated on for a large tumor in her breast. Instead of whiskey, she bit down on a silver coin and toughed it out. Many people died not from primary injuries but from gangrene and secondary complications. The connection between unwashed hands and infection was still not generally known. The only cure for gangrene was quick amputation. Experienced surgeons could saw off a leg and cauterize the stump in less than a minute.

Bloodletting or "therapeutic vampirism" was mainline medicine. Doctors had no cure for epidemics of malaria, yellow fever, and cholera and often were victims themselves. Texas towns were plagued with rats, fleas, mosquitoes, sewage, contaminated water, and dead animals decaying in the streets. In 1839 yellow fever killed one-twelfth of Houston's population and 250 people in Galveston. Common treatments were quinine, morphine, bleeding, turpentine, castor oil, camphor, ammonia, and brandy.

It was the grand age of medical quackery. Patent medicines

claimed to cure everything from baldness, "torpor of the bowels," and dropsy to "female obstruction," "loss of nature" (male libido problems), and "habitual costiveness" (constipation). Probably these preparations did make people feel better due to a potent combination of alcohol and opium. One quack remedy was the "madstone," thought to be a cure for rabies. Found in deer stomachs, the stones were probably gallstones. The "madstone" supposedly would draw out the poison from the bite of a rabid animal.

It was debatable whether the doctor or the disease would send you quicker to your grave. While some doctors like Ashbel Smith and George Cupples had earned degrees from Yale or Edinburgh, most had only haphazard training or held degrees from what today we would call diploma mills.

Conditions were not much better in Europe where medical charlatans had long been a literary motif. Molière's comedies about false doctors belong to the golden age of French theatre. The conversations of Sganarelle the quack and Géronte are classics. Géronte wonders whether the heart is on the left side of the body and the liver on the right. To which Sganarelle famously reponds: "It used to be that way. But we have changed all that and now practice medicine in a totally new way."

Sganarelle's words were ahead of history; fortunately for us, modern doctors do indeed practice medicine in a totally new way. As a result, today the average American life span is more than double what it was in 1840.

Article 47: Last Picture Show?

Growing up in the rural South had its tough side. But later I learned that growing up anywhere and everywhere has its own poverty and richness. Here I want to talk about some of the compensations.

Although life was hard, there were ways to escape dreary reality, alternate universes I could visit, there to converse in books with friends—maybe my best ones—and relive in histories "the greatness that was Greece and the grandeur that was Rome" and experience, in the words of Wordsworth, "old, unhappy, far-off things and battles long ago." Then in my own time and place I could fish and explore caves and forests. Often I carried a rifle with me, not to hunt but to feel dangerous.

But the most pleasurable excursions away from the humdrum were the picture shows, as we called them. From the start I was addicted to movies and missed no chance to see one—if I could scrounge up a ride to town and twenty-five cents for admission. Then, for an hour and a half, I would experience what the phenomenologists call an *epoché*, a suspension of common life.

I distinctly recall the first time the spell broke in the middle of a very bad film. Suddenly I noticed my surroundings and recognized, as though coming out of a hypnotic trance, the real world. I was not happy, the magic was fractured. It seemed, to quote Wordsworth again, that "there hath passed away a glory from the earth."

Afterwards I became more discriminating in my choice of movies. My enthusiasm continued and in diminishing stages still does. At its best, I think the cinema was a marvelous addition to the world's art forms, rivaling and in its impact surpassing ballet, opera, and theatre as the most human forms of aesthetics.

Except that in recent times I note that movies have gone dark and gloomy, reminiscent of European cinema of the 1930s. Is Hollywood afraid of light and beauty? Once upon a time I and millions like me went to the movies to see a world more luminous and beautiful than common life. Today I come out of the theater relieved to see that the sky is still blue, the sun still shines, and most people don't walk around in heavy body armor killing every person who peers around a corner or carry weapons powerful enough to demolish whole cities.

Maybe you know the answer to my question: how is it that in these apocalyptic films there never seems to be a shortage of ammunition or fuel for the monstrous vehicles that explode in horrific collisions? In a world in total panic and collapse somebody, it seems, is still turning out bullets and refining petroleum. Apparently industrialized capitalism thrives even as whole cities are being blown to smithereens. Maybe the system is more resilient than we think.

Hollywood is losing me. I wonder if I am about to see my last picture show.

Article 48:
A Post-legal Era?

King Hammurabi of Babylon gets credit for the first code of 282 laws in 1754 B.C. These dealt largely with retaliatory justice, including the famous injunction, "an eye for an eye and a tooth for a tooth" that was incorporated in the Bible. The language sounds harsh to modern readers, but the intent was to limit punishment to the scope of the crime. To lose an eye or a tooth was not a sufficient reason to kill the offending person.

Before there were laws and enforcers, justice was a personal matter. It was up to each man or his kinsman to avenge personal insults or injuries. There are many examples of this personal retaliatory justice in Homer, the Bible and other ancient writings. We see it in the chivalric honor code of the Middle Ages, and it persisted into modern times. Two of the American Founding Fathers, Alexander Hamilton and Aaron Burr, fought a duel in which Hamilton died. The retaliatory code was reborn on the lawless American frontier and still resonates strongly in the modern American psyche.

As the frontier stage of American civilization passed, "frontier justice" gave way to the legal system of courts and law enforcement. If retaliatory justice was a personal matter for men, the new premise of civilization was an impartial matter of law, not of men. Henceforth people were not to take justice in their own hands but to leave it to the agencies of law and order.

But in recent decades there has arisen a perception that we have law without order, crime without punishment, and punishment without crime. There is a cynical view that law is the instrument of the rich and clever whereby they unjustly manipulate and bully the poor and the plain. At the same time, we notice an increasing indifference for certain laws at a much higher level. Recently, I read that more than twenty states have decided to ignore Federal law on several issues. And so-called "sanctuary cities" disregard both state and federal statutes, adhering instead to their municipal guidelines.

In my youth I dared not target practice with my rifle on rural mailboxes. Not that any official was watching; it was simply that the mailboxes were supposedly under federal protection, and our fearful respect for federal law was second only to our reverence for things sacred. We obeyed even when no one was watching.

Today this disregard for human law means that while a residue of fear persists because the power to punish still exists, respect for the legal system has declined markedly. Once a sign of excellence, a federal label now symbolizes waste and inefficiency to many Americans. Today boys vandalize mailboxes whenever they please.

Have matters gone beyond the point of legal control? Are we entering a post-legal era? If so, then probably we can expect a resurgence of retaliatory justice, to put it in today's jargon, an era of "road rage" on steroids.

Article 49:
Separation of Powers

Thomas Jefferson gave us the wording of one of the most debated topics of our time: Separation of Church and State. There are three oddities and certain possible consequences of the controversy. First, Jefferson himself was not a Christian, but a Deist in the mold of Bolingbroke, Shaftesbury, and other European and American Enlightenment thinkers, including, briefly, Benjamin Franklin. Jefferson rejected such creedal tenets as the messiahship of Jesus and the belief that he was the incarnate Son of God. He redacted from his own Bible references to miracles and was always reluctant to discuss his religious beliefs.

Second, though now firmly established as a principle of American governance, the wording "Separation of Church and State" is not found in the Constitution itself. President Jefferson mentioned it specifically in a letter to the Connecticut Baptist Association in 1802 in which he vigorously defended church autonomy and religious liberty. It reflects wording in the constitution that prohibits government from enacting any law that interferes with the free exercise of religious practices and beliefs.

Yet in the slow spin of history in which individual freedom and political absolutism alternate in predominance, this early Jeffersonian and constitutional determination to protect religion is now declining. The Church is increasingly confined to its sanctuary, which effectively bars it from social interaction and prohibits it, under pain of penalizations and loss of privileges, from preaching certain topics which many Christians traditionally considered doctrinal. In other words, government can, at its discretion, coerce the Church, but the Church may not legitimately affect political life.

The dogma of separation lately begins to point to an eventual doctrine of elimination. In America this tendency has its roots in the public assumption—held by Christians and non-Christians alike—that everything secular falls under state jurisdiction. In successive stages since the founding of America—and in reality, since the Reformation—the Church has come to be narrowly confined, whereas the State has grown to include almost everything else.

This trend is not primarily the work of evil people, as offended Christians often protest, but is an inertial and impersonal social force that continues along a foreseeable trajectory. Indeed, many of its human enforcers are themselves Christians. Nevertheless, persecutions, church closures, and incarcerations may lie ahead.

Naturally, the avowed enemies of the Church take advantage of this movement. But neither defenders nor opponents of Christianity have seen that beyond the deconstruction of the Church an even bolder ambition appears: nothing less than the elimination of all religions.

Consider the logic: if anti-religious forces can eliminate Christianity with all its theological depth, cultural riches, and prestige in the modern world, then it is unlikely that other religions could long survive. Hence the intensity of opposition to Christianity. For if it perishes, probably other religions would also disappear. For centuries critics of religion have believed that if the world were rid of priests, popes, and worshippers, humanity could rise to a more enlightened world order.

Article 50:
Life in the Middle Ages

The Middle Ages were less male-dominated than later centuries. The respective skills the sons and daughters of common families learned from parents and relatives were the extent of their education. Nor did their lives greatly diverge with maturity and marriage but continued in the rough equality that prevails when the sexes labor together in the hard toils of livelihood. There were no isolated families or lonely people. These are modern phenomena. Safety lay in numbers. In medieval times common people, or serfs, all lived communally on self-sustaining manors, or plantations, subject to an overlord to whom they pledged fealty and services in return for his protection. This tightknit society basically consisted of three classes: those who worked (serfs), those who prayed (clergy), and those who fought (the lord and his knights.)

But time brought changes. The growth of cities and universities in the later Middle Ages created a gradual polarization of the sexes. For centuries women continued to live their stable, unchanging lives. They ran their households and taught children proper manners, language, stories, songs, games, dress, prohibitions, and religious beliefs. Even today these elements remain the primary meaning of "education" in several European languages.

As vocations and opportunities expanded, many young men found it necessary to supplement this basic education with guild apprenticeships and for those more intellectually gifted university studies. Literacy in Latin ceased to be a rarity and became a requirement in the professions. In the universities a growing intellectual class learned the intoxicating ideas of science, rhetoric, logic, music, politics, art, and philosophy. Although men retained their traditional religious faith, it was overshadowed by new theories and doctrines. Meanwhile, women, who would have no access to universities until several centuries later, continued to live the calmer life of traditional behaviors and beliefs.

Seduced by emerging arts and sciences, man found in faith-anchored woman a serene pace of life that contrasted with the frenzy of his ambitions. Her very reticence was alluring. Not that she was weak: anchored in immemorial beliefs, woman often proved stronger in the face of calamity and heartbreak. If man fought for the faith, woman lived it, as a fundamental component of the culture she transmitted to new generations. She could be counted on to hold things together, and because she could, she was. If man was obsessed with theology, philosophy, law, politics, war and conquest, woman was devoted to the timeless tasks of hearth and home and derived strength from the consolations of faith, family, and friends.

How often man set out to master the world, and nearly as often he returned, careworn and wounded, to the charms and comforts offered by strong and gentle woman who cared so little for his grandiose ideas and so much for him. It was no coincidence that the great age of lyricism and chivalry arose when women embodied a nobler way of life and lived it with an unmatched grace.

Article 51:
A Matter of Time

Almost anybody can tell us what time it is, but not even the smartest people can explain what time itself is. Philosopher Martin Heidegger says in his book *Being and Time* that it is the "horizon of every understanding and interpretation of being," which tells us a bit less than we already know. Science fiction writer Ray Cummings once quipped: "Time is what keeps everything from happening at once."

In a controversial essay published in 1908, J.M.E. McTaggart argued that because events cannot change their tense, we are left with two possibilities: either time does not exist or it is static and does not pass. Philosophers of time have argued ever since about his contradictory ideas. Novelist Eduardo Mallea and poet Austin Dobson side with McTaggart's second premise by telling us that it is not time that passes, but we who pass through time. Could they be right?

Theoretical physicist Stephen Hawkings' popular book *A Brief History of Time* deals with so many fascinating topics that we almost forget that he talks very little of time itself, and then mostly about the temporal relationship between cosmic objects. When the Universe has expanded beyond all measurable distance, time for all theoretical purposes will have ceased.

Philosophers of time offer several ideas about how it should be divided. One group (Quine, Grunbaum, Smart) favor what is called "eternalism," or "block theory of time." They argue that past, present, and future are our subjective interpretations and that time is one and indivisible. Another group (Parmenides, Duns Scotus, Prior) are "presentists." For them only the present time is real. The past is a dimension of the present, and the future is only temporal potentiality. A third group (Aristotle, Broad, Jeffrey) believe in the "growing past." For them the past is real and grows as present time flows into it. Future time is still unreal. This is the commonsense idea of time. In relativity theory time is called the fourth dimension. The idea fascinates but only adds to the mystery.

An ancient theory of time, the Kalam Cosmological Argument, updated by philosopher William L. Craig, is an argument for a beginning of time. If the Universe were infinitely old, then as Set Theory demonstrates, time could never result in the present moment. You cannot count your way out of infinity.

So what is time? Who knows? I once wrote that "time is the duration of space, and space is the fullness of time." My point was that time and space are inseparably defined by each other as part of the cosmic fabric. But I would not bet the farm on my statement. Time baffles the best minds. St. Augustine described the perplexity: "What, then, is time? If no one asks me, I know; but if I wish to explain it to one who asks, I know not."

Article 52: The Wild Card of Chance

Most of us have a healthy skepticism regarding long-range predictions. And no wonder; nearly all predictions made centuries or even decades ago turned out to be false. Predictive science, if it can be called that, is probably the most unreliable of human endeavors. It is based on the false assumption that the main course of events will continue, disregarding the cumulative, mutative effects of chance that by definition cannot be predicted.

During the Cold War anguished prophets with impressive scientific credentials assured us that the doomsday clock of nuclear annihilation was only minutes from striking midnight. But midnight never came. What happened? Simply put, chance intervened to demolish certainties and alter events.

"Chance" and its equivalents in several languages contain the idea of "falling." German *Zufall* and English "befall" convey the same root meaning of the unexpected that falls in our pathway. In what may be the chanciest of all life's unplanned happenings, we "fall" in love.

The wild card of chance breaks up our well-laid schemes, restores us to freedom, and disrupts the humdrum routine of life. This restoration of freedom has a nice ring to it because it has long enjoyed a favorable press. But freedom can also be perilous and terrifying. War, pestilence, and penury may demolish old restrictions but leave us in despair.

Other chance events are pleasant. At a party we had not planned to attend perhaps we shall meet the person who will become the love of our life, or through an unplanned experience we may discover our true vocation.

Chance also plays out on a far grander scale. Think of the consequences that flowed from a certain Jewish teacher instructing his disciples on the dusty roads of Galilee, or the unforeseen results of garrulous Greek thinkers arguing philosophy on Mars Hill in Athens, or the transcendent aftermath of white sails rising on the blue Caribbean horizon in 1492. We ponder similar surprises chance may be about to launch in our own time.

If life consisted only of "acts" and "facts, then there would be nothing we could call chance. We would say simply that what happens, happens. We cannot control chance but we may humanize it by creatively weaving it into the fabric of our life. In large measure the difference between success and failure in life lies in our response to the chance events that are certain to happen but always at an uncertain hour.

But in themselves such encounters are not enough. It takes courage to accept them, for often they come entangled with fazing complications. Nothing is sadder than the love we lost because of paralyzing timidity or the vocation that slipped away because we were not bold enough to seize it at the high tide of opportunity.

It is a mystery but also a truth that chance favors the brave, and as the poet Terence reminds us, if we face it resolutely it will sometimes reward us with things we dare not even hope for.

Article 53:
To Bathe or not to Bathe

Louis XIV, France's greatest monarch (1643-1715), reigned for over 72 years and in all that time bathed only twice. They called him the "Sun King" (*Le Roi Soleil*), but sun and water hardly ever touched his rancid torso. His physicians advised against bathing for health reasons, and Louis himself said that bathing "disturbed" him. Not by coincidence, his personal squalor combined with his womanizing ways helped popularize deodorants, perfumes, and scented cloths to mask the odors in his court. Not that it helped very much. The Russian ambassador to France remarked that "His majesty stunk like a wild animal." The Russians themselves bathed more often than Western Europeans, who denounced them as "perverts."

Louis was not the only ruler comfortable with filthiness. Queen Elizabeth I of Spain said that she bathed only twice: the day she was born and the day she was married. Aristocratic Europeans bathed only a few times a year and most commoners not at all. Early Europeans had bathed regularly, but with the coming of Christianity, Church leaders denounced bathing because they believed it drew sinful attention to the body and encouraged promiscuity. There was a saying: "Saintliness smells bad."

Southern Europeans had cleaner habits, particularly those with a lingering Roman influence or areas such as southern Spain and Portugal with a Moslem impact. Some Iberian cities regulated bathing: men on certain days, women on others, with fines for violators. This cleanliness paid off during the Plague that struck Europe in 1348 and killed perhaps a fourth of the northern European population. Southern Europe fared better, probably because of better hygiene. But centuries would pass before the link between cleanliness and health became known.

Americans were heirs to the dirty ways of their European ancestors. It has been estimated that fewer than one in ten Americans bathed even once a year in the early 1800s. Nor were Texans of that time—or later—wasteful with soap and water. Not that most used soap when they bathed; it was reserved for washing clothes. A brisk rubdown with a coarse towel loosened the caked-on body dirt. Ironically, many young boys were cleaner than girls and adults because they swam in creeks.

Although these attitudes lingered into the twentieth century, a new hygienic philosophy was expressed in the saying: "cleanliness is next to godliness." My mother was a devout believer in the modern credo. I am sure that as children my siblings and I had the cleanest ears, bodies, faces, and fingernails in the area due to her vigorous scrubbings. Her mania for cleanliness caused me at times to envy members of the old school of nasties, two of whom it was whispered with awe and repugnance had never taken a bath. We stared at them from a distance, for like the Russian ambassador at King Louis XIV's court, we learned that you did not want to stand too close to them.

Article 54: Voting Old Style

Maybe it's true that the more things change the more they stay the same. Charles Taylor of Nacogdoches wrote in 1839: "Nothing is now talked of but the approaching elections. I was present yesterday at a 'stump speechification.' There was much recrimination and but little discrimination between the Candidates."

It was the era of "Jacksonian Democracy" when voting was changing in two ways. First, suffrage was being extended to new classes of people (though not to women and minorities), and, second, written votes were replacing the old system of voice voting.

Viva voce, or voice voting, was a rough and sometimes violent expression of democracy. A reflection of the widespread illiteracy of earlier times, voice voting was anything but today's written "secret ballot, which did not become standard until after the Civil War. Once a man shouted out his choice he became a target of those favoring the other candidate. And since elections were an all-male business, drunkenness, challenges, and fights were common. A very old man I knew claimed to recall the scene. He would trace a circle on the ground and dare any man of opposing views to step inside it and settle with their fists differences raised by their vote.

Suffrage broadened greatly when requirements such as ownership of property, minimum tax payment, and length of residency were eased or abolished. Approximately 80% of the eligible white men voted in the 1840 election.

During the Texas Republic intense campaigning by

candidates was uncommon. There were no primary elections or nominating conventions. A candidate's name would be placed in nomination by friends. A resolution of nomination would be sent to newspapers. The nominee would then "sacrificially" agree to serve at the request of citizens. Candidates were expected to attend every ball and wedding in his county. Francis Lubbock, candidate for the clerkship of Harris County in 1840, handed out cut tobacco to gain support. It was customary for a candidate, including Lubbock, to place a barrel of whiskey for voters in a local store. Those who accepted a drink were expected to vote for the candidate who supplied it.

Mudslinging was common then as now. Dr. Alonzo Sweitzer called opponent Ben McCullogh a "moral coward" and "sneaking skulker." McCullogh won anyway and challenged Sweitzer to a duel. He refused, stating that McCullough was not his equal. McCullough responded: "As you will not fight when you have a fair and honorable opportunity, I cannot afford to shoot you down like a dog. I must content myself by pronouncing you a black-hearted cowardly villain." Later he dueled Colonel Reuben Ross, Sweitzer's second, and sustained a wound that never fully healed.

Personalities, not principles, decided elections. As one Texan put it in 1843, "We here in Texas had nothing to do with parties in the United States. We were Sam Houston or anti-Sam Houston; Eastern Texas was largely for and Western Texas against him."

Much has changed, but much remains the same.

Article 55:
Life in Three Centuries

Recently I visited my Appalachian birthplace and without fail the experience had its disturbing effect. I have spent many more years here than there, and with each return visit I must slip back into an alter ego I left behind all those years ago. I need that person and the perspective of those early times to reintroduce me to my first world. Since then I have earned degrees, learned a few languages, read and written books, taught at universities, and most of all, made a living and raised a family. To go back to that first world involves a strange metamorphosis. I welcome it but it does not readily welcome me. We are a bit standoffish with each other. To put it paradoxically, my old world and I are familiar strangers.

The sensation always brings up a question. Who would I be if I had remained in that environment? A celebrated philosopher once said, "I am I and my circumstance." A dramatic way of putting it, but it means the world we live in forms the other half of our being. By reentering it I glimpse the life I could have lived and the person I might have been.

I grew up surrounded by elderly relatives born far back in the 1800s. Their ideas, language and outlook became mine, and probably more than I know, remain so today. In lower Appalachia we had no electricity, telephones, automobiles, radios, computers and much less television. We walked, rode horses, or drove wagons to visit, attend church and do business. But if today we define that bygone era by the things we lacked, we can also remember it by the things we lost. Calendars said it was the 20th century, but in effect and in form, we were people of the 1800s and heirs of earlier centuries. We rose with crowing roosters, worked and played by daylight, cooked and ate ancestral food, farmed as our forefathers had farmed, and after a brief interval of reading or conversing by lamplight or fireplace, retired to night's velvety quiet dominion. By today's standards, it was a supremely personal world dominated by human faces and spoken words.

Then the aggressive 20th century began its invasion. First came electricity. I shall never forget the euphoria I experienced at my first sight of an electric light bulb dangling from a cord. Like a crazed moth, I ran circles around it until I was exhausted from the splendor. Ancient cars began to appear on our muddy, rutted roads and for a time wagon ruts and car tracks vied for predominance. Then after WWII, the 20th century triumphed; the wagons suddenly disappeared and the old world was gone. Eventually the tortured 20th century ended and the terroristic 21st replaced it.

Exaggerating to make the point, I claim to have lived in three centuries. I treasure them all impartially, but nostalgia, that mellow distillation of time, pleads mightily for the first.

Article 56: Revolutionary Shortcuts

Nearly everybody admires revolutionaries, as we admire tigers, crocodiles and sharks, but we prefer to watch them from a safe distance. Nobody wants to meet up with one.

Classic revolution may be described as a repudiation of history and a shortcut to the future. The Quixotic idealism that revolution evokes rides on the hope that a wayward nation can correct its mistakes, as a crook can mend his ways, and live a better life. But as the remedial methodology of impatient and exasperated people, revolutionary outcomes are many times no better—and often worse—than the abuses they set out to remedy. Many of us know from experience that shortcuts and quick remedies often leave us far from where we thought we were going. Don Quixote began with noble intentions, but in many cases he made things worse than before.

We describe nearly everything under the sun as a revolution. To hear people tell it, there are revolutions going on all around us: in sports, politics, medicine, technology, education, and science, to mention only a few. You name the area and chances are it is in the middle of its own revolution. Happily, these metaphorical revolutions do not involve killing people.

The futility of many—not to say most—revolutions does not seem to deter revolutionaries in the least, nor does it lessen the general enthusiasm in our time for new ones. I have written before about the French Revolution, the grandfather and inspiration of all the later ones. Yet by objective standards it was a failure. France survived the Napoleonic carnage and tyranny but was never again the predominant power it had been under the monarchy.

Three less spectacular revolutionary movements in our Western Hemisphere, Colombia, Cuba and Mexico reveal the contradictory outcome of revolutions. In all three the prevailing idealism was the same and the problems were similar. But none turned out as hoped. In Colombia, fighting dragged on for over sixty years, costing the lives of hundreds of thousands of Colombian people. The spark that set off the conflagration—the assassination of a popular president in 1948—later was submerged in other griefs and causes. Only now, decades later, has the killing stopped. The revolution failed from fatigue and age. Revolution is a young man's dream but an old man's nightmare.

The Cuban Revolution was a response to dictatorial abuses but from the start subservient to a foreign ideology. As promised, the Cuban revolutionaries abolished the former tyrannical regime, then in typical fashion replaced it with even greater tyranny.

It is interesting to note that Mexico ended its revolutionary period in a counterrevolutionary way by trying to institutionalize revolution as a political party (The Institutional Revolutionary Party, or PRI in Spanish). It was the political equivalent of trying to square the circle. Like hurricanes, revolutions cannot be permanent. The same temperament that drives revolutionaries to excel at destruction causes them to fail at the daily grind of governing.

Article 57:
More on Revolution

Revolution is one of those overworked words we barely notice anymore. We are used to hearing everything from cars to cosmetics described as revolutionary. But I feel a shiver of dismay when I hear that a real revolution has broken out somewhere. I'll tell you why.

Revolutions have nearly always enjoyed a favorable press. The granddaddy of them all, the French Revolution of 1789, even had at least a half century of prior praise before it engulfed France and Europe in a frenzy of executions and wars. Voltaire, Diderot, Rousseau, Montesquieu, Holbach, and others—none of whom lived to see the results of their efforts—eagerly prepared the way with diatribes against the *Ancien Régime*, meaning the Monarchy, the Nobility, and the Church. Above all, with irrepressible enthusiasm they championed the ideals of liberty, equality, and fraternity.

The problem with revolutions is that instead of establishing freedom, they customarily end in tyranny. It was true of the French, the Russian, the Cuban, and others of lesser profile. Napoleon cleverly steered popular enthusiasm for the French Revolution to his own imperialistic schemes and plunged Europe into protracted wars. As for the French themselves, they did not gain the desired freedoms until 1830 during the reign of Louis Philippe, forty-one years after the Revolution.

But just a minute, you remind me, what about the American Revolution of 1776? Didn't it deliver on its promises? Indeed, it did, perhaps because it was not a revolution at all, at least not in the radical French or Russian sense. The Americans had no intention of abolishing religion, adopting a new judicial code, or restructuring society. English Common Law remained the foundation of the American Legal system. Religion continued unmolested. The Americans revolted because they wanted to live under just laws with fair representation and equitable taxation but without the burdensome decrees of King George III.

Despite the failures of revolutionaries since 1789, the modern media generally applaud them. Che Guevara, who died a revolutionary failure in Bolivia, lives on as a heroic symbol of defiance and rebellion, especially among the young. Why this continuing approval of movements that consistently fail? I have said one key word already: enthusiasm. The other is exasperation. Nothing is more stirring than fighting for mankind's highest ideals, and nothing motivates revolutionaries more than exasperation with unjust systems. Revolutionaries are not gradualists but impatient people who want immediate changes.

But enthusiasm and exasperation are no match for the cunning betrayals that routinely turn revolutionary dreams into nightmares. The longing for freedom is part of the human condition, but so also is the lust for power. This is why the worst enemies of revolution are not the original oppressors but Judas betrayers in the revolutionary ranks. The great challenge remains of finding ways to channel this impatient idealism into lasting benefits for the people. The prospects are not promising. Revolutionaries often win the war but as consistently squander the victory.

Article 58: Inventing the Flat Earth

Most of us learned in school that medieval people believed in a flat earth. We read of sailors, including some of Columbus' crew, terrified of sailing too far out and plunging over the edge of the world.

No doubt many people of that time did believe the world was flat. Today some may still. But not medieval philosophers, theologians, and scholars, who knew better for reasons I shall give later. And not experienced sailors such as Columbus who were accustomed to seeing shorelines and vessels dip below the horizon.

American writer Washington Irving helped popularize the flat earth myth and the hypothetical terror aboard Columbus' vessels in his novel *A History of the Life and Voyages of Christopher Columbus* (1828).

French historian Jean-Antoine Letronne wrote in 1834 that for a thousand years the Catholic Church persecuted men who denied the world was flat. English philosopher Thomas Hobbes made similar charges in the seventeenth century. The cumulative effect was that by the end of the nineteenth century the flat earth myth was firmly fixed in modern thinking.

The only thing wrong is that these claims are false. In *Inventing the Flat Earth: Columbus and Modern Historians*, Jeffrey Burton Russell exposes the flat earth myth not as ignorance or bad science but as a modern fabrication. Yet it has a tenacious grip on our thinking, probably because it props up other stereotypes about the Middle Ages.

Far from persecuting people for denying a flat earth, the

Catholic Church had always taught that it was round. Authorities such as St. Augustine and St. Thomas Aquinas described a spherical world. Aristotle, the Church's ultimate authority in matters of science, declared the earth to be round, and until Copernicus his theories were considered to be infallible.

Letronne's prestige was so great that he did not have to cite sources to back his claims. And a good thing for him, too, for there is no record of any such persecutions he could have cited. As for Irving, his novel about Columbus was fictional but came to be treated as factual.

Before the Christian era, the classical Greek thinkers already knew the world was round and with ingenious experiments carried out in Egypt were even able to calculate its approximate circumference. Although Columbus lacked this precise knowledge of the earth's dimensions, he knew the earth was round but underestimated its size.

There are other medieval writings about a round earth. In 1265 Brunet Latini wrote in his *Livres dou Tresor* (Books of the Treasure): "In this, Nature was provident inasmuch as she made the Earth completely round." He goes on to say with surprising accuracy that the Sun, stars, and outer planets are much larger than the Earth, whereas the Moon, Mercury, and Venus are smaller.

Both Latini and celebrated medieval traveler Marco Polo endorsed the round earth theory by reasoning that if a man started west and nothing impeded him, he would eventually circle the globe and return from the east.

For several years Russell's book made little headway against the flat earth fiction. But now, as the truth slowly comes to light, translations of Russell's book are beginning to appear. The whole myth of the flat earth is a tale of malice and deception on a vast scale but far too long to tell here.

Article 59:
The Elephant in the Room

Among the many sources of problems is the unnoticed "elephant in the room" we call laziness. It misses deadlines, disregards safety protocols, and explains a multitude of failures that seemingly have no rational explanation. When tragedies occur as a result, we hear pledges that "it will never happen again." But lazy people are forgetful people who put responsibility at the bottom of their priorities. Resolve soon fades and the tragic cycle recurs.

The effects of laziness are everywhere: messages that go unanswered; employees who give misleading information instead of checking for accuracy; experts who falsify tests rather than running them; attorneys who fail to show for court dates; mechanics who forget to put new oil in the engine after an oil change; and ministers who "wing" their sermons.

Professors cope with student laziness in bad papers and failed tests. No surprise there. Lazy students have been around forever. But it can go both ways when professors do not update or even prepare their lectures. Years ago on a scheduled official visit to a certain Central American university, I arrived at the appointed hour—to an empty building. Apparently it was common, I learned later, for students and professors not to attend classes. The students got credit for courses and the professors received their salary. Finally, I located a forlorn secretary who called university officials—also absent—with the alarming news that a scheduled foreign visitor was on campus. They came running armed with more phony excuses than I could count. For all practical purposes it was a "phantom" university.

But these examples pale in comparison with laziness at much higher levels of medicine and research. In a recent book, one of America's most distinguished medical diagnosticians took senior doctors to task for depending on patient charts drawn up by interns. If these sleep-deprived and inexperienced youngsters make diagnostic mistakes, these are routinely passed along. In many cases, the indignant author claims, senior physicians do not bother to recheck the initial charts for themselves. For him it was simple laziness at a dangerous level.

In the humanities many lazy scholars do not read primary sources but repeat what other writers have said. But these in turn may have copied even earlier writers. In some cases plagiarized inaccuracies continue for generations. The Internet has only magnified the problem. Since many American scholars do not learn other languages, they must depend on translations. But because translation is extremely labor-intensive and poorly paid work, many important writings are not translated into English. And even when adequate, translations are hardly ever as good as the originals. Laziness abounds, but we hesitate to call the elephant by its name.

Article 60:
Neither Here nor There

Well, I finally figured it out: some time back I must have died. It's the only logical explanation for all the weird things that have been happening around here. I had read of cases similar to mine: people who died and didn't realize they were dead. But I always thought they were just stories and not real happenings. I always assumed that everybody died in the normal way, you know, with obituaries, wakes, funerals, dark clothes, and flowers, capped off with the happy news that the leadership at Universal Headquarters had promoted them to a higher level job with super benefits. Still, we missed our old buddies and though happy for them, we were saddened to tears about ourselves still stuck in our old 8 to 5 grind and unsure about our own promotion because of some mess-ups on the job that I won't go into.

I suspected something was wrong when I went into a store several months ago and couldn't get anybody's attention. Several times employees seemed to look my way, but then brushed by to wait on other customers behind me. I left the store miffed but not mystified. Even when I was alive, I had no personal presence to speak of. I could walk through police barricades and restricted sites without being noticed or challenged. People thought I belonged wherever I was, like a lizard on the fence or a fly on the wall. Come to think of it, maybe I would make a good spy. Nobody notices me, but no one bothers me either.

Other bizarre things happened. One day in a fast-food place the employees were taking everybody's order—except mine, of course. Maybe they assumed I had ordered and was waiting for my number to be called. I left hungry, already becoming convinced that I was invisible to ordinary people.

But the best evidence that I had passed away occurred at a recent family gathering. I sat in a corner and kept quiet as the young folks chattered about things I knew nothing about. I brightened, though, when the topic of history came up and was just beginning to expound on an exciting theory of early American fiscal policy when Cousin Velma came in cuddling her new kitten. With o*ohs!* and *aahs!* everybody stampeded in her direction and I was forgotten for the rest of the afternoon.

On those rare occasions when people do seem to listen when I talk about important things, like vowel shifts in Medieval Latin, would you believe that they quickly nod off into a sound sleep?

All this tells me, as I said, that somewhere along the way I must have passed away, but where I passed to I can't say. So I am writing to see if there are other people in the same quandary. I have no idea when it happened or where it leaves me. I guess you could say I am neither here nor there.

Article 61: Propaganda and Rhetoric

Although both terms have a negative image in our day, historically, propaganda and rhetoric are deeply and decisively different. Propaganda is the technique of manipulating people with artful lies and a disrespect for reality. Rhetoric, on the other hand, is the art of moving people with truth beautifully and eloquently spoken. It can be argued that truth poorly told is not fully true. Pericles, who presided over the Golden Age of Athens, said that "He who knows but does not explain himself clearly is the same as one who does not think." He who "knows" means one who knows the truth, who seizes and masters it, and does not allow empty echoes to replace reality. It is a matter of conforming language to reality so that words—precise, rigorous, brilliant and beautiful—say what they mean and mean what they say. This aesthetic principle was deeply embedded in classical Mediterranean cultures—Greek, Latin, and their descendants—less so in the Northern cultures, which generally equate truth and fact and assume that verbal beautification is cosmetic and not strictly necessary.

Both rhetoric and sophistry—an early equivalent of propaganda—were understood to mean the spoken word. The written word was decidedly secondary in the Age of Pericles and continued to be so for centuries to come. Parliament, the epitome of political life, comes from the French *parler*, meaning to speak. Language means, or used to mean, primarily spoken words. Written documents issued by Congress, Parliament, academic conferences, or seminars diminish the full content of the message, often rendering it boring, impersonal, and hard to understand. And no wonder; written words lack the personal features—intonation, pauses, gestures, smiles, frowns, emphasis, gravity, repetition, and humor—that complete understanding. Faith, the deepest form of understanding, comes from hearing, so the Scriptures tell us, not primarily from reading. Many a spell-binding sermon, college lecture, or political speech moves us far less in written versions.

In a democracy, rhetoric and propagandistic demagoguery weave a tapestry of success or failure. Political power derives ultimately not from an expression of force but from the force of expression. But if this pattern is ideal, it is not the rule. The temptation to fall back into sophistry, into demagoguery, is a political virus ever ready to sicken the body politic. It offers quick results but at an unaffordable cost. In the long run it cannot stand up to truth. For truth has its act together; it is coherent, not self-contradictory. Each truth supports and strengthens all the others. Truth is an interlocking system; demagoguery, a chaos of singularities.

We do well to remember the cited words of Pericles. He rejected muddled thinking and sought instead a rhetoric of truth and beauty. It led on to the greatness that was Classical Greece. He knew in his day, as we must now rediscover in ours, that sound thinking is the subsoil of sound politics and the prime condition of enlightened human life.

Article 62: Women in the Enlightenment

The Enlightenment, centered in eighteenth-century France, set our still-expanding agenda for the advancement of human rights in modern times, but with glaring exceptions, including the rights of women. Many of the notable male figures of the era, David Hume, Jean-Jacques Rousseau, Baron Melchior Grimm, Restif de la Bretonne, and Napoleon himself were misogynists, or woman-haters. Samia Spencer writes in her book *French Women and the Age of Enlightenment* that these men ". . . were appalled by what they viewed as the lawlessness and unruliness of at least some eighteenth-century French women." Yet despite severe legal and educational restrictions, a mesmerizing galaxy of women impacted the history of their time to a degree probably unmatched in all human history: Mme du Maine, Mme de Tencin, Mme de Pompadour, Mme d'Epinay, Mme Geoffrin, Mme du Deffand, Mlle de Lespinasse, Mme du Chatlet.

Consider some of the restrictions under which they labored. Women were barred from law and the judiciary. For the most part, they were either self-educated, or gleaned what they could, particularly Latin and mathematics, from their brothers' tutors. To cite Spencer again, "Officially, women remained an imperfect man, a weak vessel, a victim of her body in general and her uterus in particular, the equivalent of an idiot or a child." Indeed, it is debatable whether the French Revolution benefited or hindered women. There is no question that the reforms envisioned by the revolutionaries and later espoused by Napoleon created opportunities for men of the lower classes.

But some of the reforms placed further restrictions on women. For example, the closing of convents, which had provided a refuge of last resort for abused women and their children, often meant that now they had nowhere to turn. Generally speaking, the revolutionary reforms had the effect of legalizing and reinforcing what had been the social inferiority of women since the Middle Ages.

As heirs to the age-old notion of female inferiority and subordination, the Enlightenment thinkers generally continued to view women as weak, shrewish, deceitful, and morally suspect. There were some exceptions. Condorcet stands as a truly enlightened champion of women's rights. And Montesquieu, one of the leading theorists of the eighteenth century, argued forcefully but abstractly that the status of women constitutes an important measure of the freedom and advancement of civilization. In other words, no civilization can regard itself as truly enlightened if half its population is condemned to ignorance and legal neglect.

Diderot, another great theoretical thinker, also took the plight of women seriously. He recognized the social problems inherent in their condition, but remained convinced of their inferiority. As he wrote to his daughter Angélique, "External affairs are his, those of the interior are yours." Translation: you must attend to your household and leave business matters to your husband.

The Marquis de Sade acknowledged what panicked earlier Enlightenment thinkers: female eroticism. But it was left to later generations to act on that part of the human agenda.

Article 63:
Varieties of Anti-Americanism

During the era 1960-1990 Western Europe displayed an anti-Americanism that at times and in some countries came close to unvarnished hatred. First noted among post-World War II intellectuals, philosophers and certain political leaders, it spread by contagion to universities and labor unions, culminating in the 1968 student and worker demonstrations in Paris. The disorganized protests soon collapsed, but the overt hostility toward the United States lingered until the demise of the Soviet Union in 1990. Vestiges of it still remain among generations that came of age in the heyday of anti-American sentiment.

At first, American reaction was disbelief, then perplexity, and finally anger. Americans could not understand the hostile feelings of their old allies. Hadn't the Americans rescued them three times within a fifty-year period? First, from Nazi tyranny, second, from economic ruin through the Marshall Plan, and third, from probable annexation by the Soviet Union.

When it first appeared, many Americans saw anti-Americanism as the despicable payback of ungrateful people. As a result, a matching, but milder, anti-Europeanism arose. There are, or have been, several varieties of anti-American sentiment. Here I suggest four. (1) political: in the case of French President Charles de Gaulle, his anti-American bias apparently was based on a perceived national decline. And the same was true of other European powers, including Great Britain. For centuries France and its neighbors—particularly Great Britain—took turns dictating the fate of the modern world. The British took their relative decline in stride and deferred without political handwringing to the United States. But De Gaulle, smarting over the decline of France, dreamed of leading a pan-Latin coalition. It failed because France lacked the means to achieve it. (2) popular: ordinary Europeans came to resent hordes of American tourists that flooded Europe in the post-war years and appeared to be on the verge of swamping traditional European culture. (3) intellectual: famous European philosophers and writers with world-wide followings excoriated the United States for its opposition to Marxism. Just as notable Europeans of the eighteenth-century Enlightenment—Voltaire, Lafayette, de Tocqueville—looked west and praised the American experiment in democracy, so their twentieth-century counterparts—Russell, Sartre, Malraux—turned east and saw the hope of mankind in the Marxist paradigm. For them, the ideal of the past had become the enemy of the future.

(4) American: nowhere does anti-Americanism appear stronger and stranger than in America itself. (I omit the forms it takes in Marxist states and non-Western cultures). Imported mainly into US universities, anti-Americanism became a pervasive dogma of American intellectualism. Like certain imported plants and animals that become "invasive species" in other habitats, anti-Americanism found a congenial environment in America where it overcame mild political and religious opposition and only minimal philosophical immunity against it. With the collapse of the Soviet Union and the intellectual idealism that surrounded it, hostility toward the United States dwindled noticeably in Europe, but anti-Americanism continues to thrive in America.

Article 64:
Meditation on a Mountain Road

Recently a relative sent me a photograph of a remote road in the Smoky Mountains. For undisclosed reasons he asked me to tell him, judging by the angle in the picture, whether it showed the road going up or down a mountain or along a level stretch. Since I am no good with trick questions, the best I could do was to send back some random thoughts on the matter.

There was no traffic on the road, which reminded me that until someone applies intention or directional purpose to the scene, it remains passive and cannot be said to tend in any direction. Someone must impose purpose on the landscape in order to activate it in our understanding. The world is knowable relative to each viewer, or personally, to me. I let the world assume order and coherence relative to my purpose for it, and the world allows me within my limits to organize and carry out my intentions with the real or imaginary resources it presents. My intention might be biological, economic, spiritual, or artistic, but nothing I do exhausts the possibilities of the world I perceive. Where my intentions end, the world continues as unrealized potentiality. It is always more than we know. And best proof of its endless possibilities is the way other people and other generations see potentialities different from ours. Probably not in their most extravagant dreams could the aboriginal inhabitants of Long Island have imagined that a great future city would stand where they pitched their tents.

We may agree culturally that we see a basic telluric reality when we view this road scene. In modern times we think that the fundamental view consists of an "objective" view of things. But this is merely an inherited convention, and for that reason a limitation, perhaps ultimately a mistake. The truth is that nobody sees anything from an "objective" perspective but always from a personal viewpoint. The objective view of things is always an imaginary vision of reality, a world seen from nowhere and by nobody.

For these reasons, we cannot limit the objects or contents of our perception to a single purpose without denying the full range of their possibilities. It is the blows of a hammer, obeying a human intention, that define the hammer, not the reverse. Given other intentions, a hammer could be a toy, a religious symbol, a weapon, or a work of art.

Every place is full of possibilities awaiting our intentions so as to yield up its meanings. But our personal intention, perspective, or interpretation can never exhaust its possibilities. Which brings me to the most generous conclusion I can reach regarding this isolated mountain road. If we knew the infinite depths and riches of those places we call lonely and desolate, how could we not live in awe of creation? And how could we ever be bored in this marvelously crafted world?

Article 65: Vacations from Rationality

One of the main ways humans use their mind is looking for the means to lose it. We classify humans above animals by defining ourselves as rational beings, but then we jump at the chance to take vacations from rationality. Philosophy, the general intellectual form of logical reasoning, has existed for only about two and half millennia, and the scientific method only a few hundred years. But the primitive mind, which has been around since the world began and, according to psychologists, is still hidden in the messy mental attics of modern people, whispers to us subversively—and often persuasively—that dreams, drugs, omens, rituals, signs, superstitions, taboos, and visions are gateways to realities more meaningful and pleasurable than our rational world. Police reports and the daily news seem to confirm the premise. As a society we wage an endless but apparently losing war on hallucinogenic drugs and intoxicating drinks. The notorious failure of Prohibition is a staple of history and Hollywood.

Paleontologists tell us that narcotics are among humanity's oldest discoveries and that far back in prehistoric times our remote ancestors already knew and used most of the classic intoxicants and narcotics: alcohol, opium, datura, hashish, mushrooms, and other plants. Viniculture, or wine making, is among mankind's oldest occupations. The ancestor of modern tobacco was so potent that Native Americans smoked it ritualistically to induce visionary trances. And the quest goes on for ways to escape our logical senses. In very recent times we have added synthetic drugs to this ancient stock of mind-altering hallucinogens. The old Latin saying, *in vino veritas* (in wine there is truth) is understood lightheartedly today to mean that drunks blurt out the truth. But in prehistoric times it had a very different connotation. In states of ritual intoxication the human mind was set aside, allowing exalted prophetic religious visions and truth to emerge. Modern scholars believe that intoxicating fumes from volcanic fissures were responsible for the prophetic oracles of Delphi and similar locations in ancient Greece.

Some scholars have advanced the hypothesis that the first shelters and caves of prehistoric mankind were not residences for daily life at all, as we assume today, but rather ritual sites where certain tribal men inhaled hallucinogenic vapors that induced visions and trances. The cave art at Lascaux, Altamira, and other locations around the world may not have been art at all as we understand it today, but a dimension of prehistoric religious ritual.

Despite our differences, our existential kinship with primitive mankind is not hard to find. Vast portions of life still consist of problems that mystify and frighten us, impelling us to find ways to deal with them. Prehistoric mankind sought answers in magical rituals and hallucinogens. Today we claim to seek solutions to our problems through the application of logical, clearheaded reason. But it does not take much for us to strip away our modern veneer, leave our mind behind, and take vacations from rationality.

Article 66: Who was Shakespeare?

Truth is often larger than facts, especially when it comes to people. Take the case of William Shakespeare (1564-1616). We know where he was born, where he lived and worked, whom he married, when he died, and several other details about his life. But respected scholars have argued that this commonplace man, who perhaps knew "little Latin and less Greek," could not have been the author whom many acknowledge as the world's greatest dramatist. Similar doubts of authorship have arisen about Miguel de Cervantes (1547-1616), the matching genius of that age. Officially, they died on the same day—April 22—in 1616, but because Spain and England followed different calendars, Shakespeare really died eleven days later.

More than two centuries after Shakespeare's death, scholars began suggesting that the real author of the Shakespearean plays was Francis Bacon, possibly Christopher Marlowe, or perhaps Edward de Vere. Others have raised questions about his sexual preferences, pointing to certain torrid verses dedicated to a young man. Lately there is also renewed uncertainty about his religion. Just as Spanish Jews and Muslims were forced to convert to Catholicism or leave the country, so in the England of Shakespeare's time, where Anglicanism was the state religion, it was illegal to be Catholic. In both countries many obligatory conversions were in name only. There is controversial evidence that Shakespeare remained secretly Catholic. As for Cervantes, there are similar intriguing hints that his ancestors may have been *conversos*, that is, Jews forced to convert to Christianity.

Not everyone was impressed with Shakespeare. In the seventeenth century, the Classic Age of French theatre with Racine, Corneille, and Moliere, the French found Shakespeare too verbally violent and barbaric for their taste. Not until Voltaire, who translated bits of Shakespeare's work in 1736-38, including Hamlet's celebrated Soliloquy, did Shakespeare begin to gain acceptance in France and elsewhere. In Restoration England itself (1660-1700) Shakespeare was considered inferior to John Fletcher and Ben Jonson, and 18th century critic Thomas Rymer condemned him for his promiscuous mixture of comedy and tragedy. But the 19th century Romantics found in his enormous passions and gorgeous linguistic power a spiritual kinship with their own artistic urges.

It is interesting to note that Shakespeare and the King James Bible coincided with the arrival of the English language in North America. Both had a profound impact on the language. To Shakespeare we owe such expressions as "a tower of strength," "at one fell swoop," "play fast and loose," "in my mind's eye," "cold comfort," "a wild goose chase" and "It's Greek to me."

Famed Mexican novelist and diplomat Carlos Fuentes offered a fascinating but far-fetched comparison of Shakespeare and Cervantes. They were the same man, he says, explaining that it was not Shakespeare or Cervantes who spoke, but the spirit of genius that spoke through them. But it was a foregone conclusion that scholars would reject his assertion. (By the way, "a foregone conclusion" is another phrase that Shakespeare introduced into English.)

Article 67: Superstition

In modern times superstition has a bad press but countless practitioners. Many of us have our favorite superstitions: knocking on wood, a found heads-up penny for good luck, and mystic numerical combinations that are sure to win us the lotto. To ward off bad luck, we avoid stepping on sidewalk cracks and turn back if a black cat crosses our road. Coaches wear the same hat or socks they had on at a winning game. And think of the bad luck that comes from breaking a mirror. Then there is unlucky Friday 13th (or Tuesday 13th in Hispanic countries).

What we call superstition today was known as *deisidaimonia*, or "god-fearing" in Classical times. The old pagan gods—our fairytale sprites and demons—were considered to be enemies and ever ready to torment mankind with curses and hexes. Religion consisted mainly of ways to appease them and to persuade them to vex one's enemies instead, much like Voodoo and similar practices today. At first the Romans considered both Judaism and Christianity to be sacrilegious insults to the pantheon of Roman gods. By the fifth century, however, when Christianity had become the official religion of the Roman Empire, all non-Christian religions were classified as paganist superstitions.

Despite its official standing, Christianity was never able to rid itself entirely of pagan symbols and beliefs inherited from pre-Christian cults. Ghosts and goblins live on in milder forms at Halloween, and countless people still carry good luck charms in pockets and purses and refuse to open umbrellas indoors.

But before dismissing all superstitions, consider some positive things about them. First, superstitions are archly human. Apparently, animals are not superstitious at all, even though in the wild they live in fearful alertness and often stark terror. Since superstition was a belief-system with its own rules of logic for dealing with forces greater than human strength, it implied a degree of self-awareness that was not merely animalistic but recognizably human. At first, mankind expressed its envy of stronger animals with imitative masks, dances, and totemic kinships. But the second stage was more remarkable: humanity's perception that it lived in a realm of unseen beings with powers not only greater but different in nature from human strength. With this realization, mankind moved beyond the physical into the metaphysical, from sight humanity progressed to insight, advancing from a dread of malignant sprites to a belief in the liberating human spirit. In successive stages of enlightenment, humanity recalibrated life, centering it increasingly on rational discernment and less on irrational fear. The process was long, often regressive, and still unfinished. Superstition was an important but limited step on the way from animal primitivism to the higher stages of theology, philosophy, and science. But since we seldom cease being entirely what we once were completely, we still preserve relics of humanity's superstitious past, as attached to them as adults are to their childhood toys.

Article 68: Sentimental Geography

Call them Susan and Bill: two young people in a city that to our disinterested eye seems like many others. Except that looks are deceiving. The lyrics of an old song, "On the Street Where You Live," describe the real city. Bill sings of his rapturous feelings as he walks along the street where Susan lives. He has walked this way often, but always before it was an ordinary street in an ordinary world. Now all that was drab glows with a halo of happiness and harmony. Bill is in love.

We are tempted to ask, so what? Hasn't this happened to millions of people before? No, love cannot be generic or transferable. Real love is always a new story. Every love is a first love, every love is an only love.

Realists would argue that the physical city is the same as it always was, and idealists might add that Bill's fancies exist only in his mind. No, the real city is human, not merely brick and buildings but a dynamic sum of many lives and generations incrementally relived in each era. His love for Susan has sentimentally elevated the city's physical geography to a higher dimension. If he knows that Susan is in a certain place, then the longest road to her becomes the shortest distance. But his nearest destination is immeasurably remote if she is not there. For Bill, the places where she has been, the people she knows, and the things she has touched become hallowed above all others. She leaves a magical trail. No wonder lovers borrow so many metaphors from sacred literature.

Resemblances jolt him like an electric current. Bill sees a woman approaching and his heart leaps. Is it Susan? Then his hope subsides when he sees a face and eyes not nearly so beautiful, features not nearly so perfect, and gestures that profane Susan's graceful manner. He experiences a fleeting disappointment. The world contains so many counterfeits.

But then a tragedy occurs: Bill learns that Susan has gone away. The glory fades and the city takes on mournful hues. Will she ever return? The separation of lovers by distance or death is an ancient theme in literature and life. Love is happiness but it does not always end happily. What will Bill do if Susan never returns? In his pain, he can only search for her and agree with the poet: *Behold the suffering of love/That knows no other cure/but the beloved's presence and figure.*

This only Bill knows: with Susan he found the beauty and meaning of his life. With her he became the man he was meant to be, and becoming who we are meant to be is happiness. This is why he would not exchange his love, tragic or not, for any other option. As Tennyson said, *tis better to have loved and lost than never to have loved at all.*

Article 69:
The Westward Urge

Horace Greeley gets credit for the celebrated advice, "Go west, young man, go west," but newspaperman John Soule actually wrote it in 1851. Greeley tried all his life to set the record straight, but the public disregarded his disclaimers and he was forever stuck with it.

The advice was unnecessary in any case. People felt the lure of the west long before either man—or the United States itself—was born. Already noticeable in old Europe, the westward wave accelerated when Europeans reached North America and continued on to the Pacific coast and beyond.

Today the westward urge is still alive, less perhaps geographically than in cultural patterns. Sociologists tell us that given equal space on all sides American cities will build to the west and decline to the east. Urban renewal projects intended to rebuild the east side of American cities usually fail or produce mediocre results. The reason: who wants to be left in the grimy east when everything is moving to the glamorous west?

The east-west dynamics has impacted American English. We still say "out west" but "back east." "Back east" sounds vaguely regressive, a return to old things already tried and done. On the other hand, the west has always been one part geography and two parts possibility. It is the limitless horizon that separates the real world from the ideal. Swinburne called it "The bountiful infinite West." And in more homespun language Arthur Chapman offers this description: "Out where the handclasp's a little stronger/ Out where the smile dwells a little longer/ That's where the West begins."

The east-west dynamics is also evident in certain other American countries settled by westward-leaning Europeans. Social scientists note that as Brazilian cities are still growing on the west side, the eastern districts are already becoming slums. This feature is less pronounced in other Ibero-American countries that lack the giant east-west geographical profile of the US or Brazil. The Russians used to complain that while the American West got all the glory and romance, their own eastern surge into Siberia was just as meaningful. Perhaps, but it seems that not even the Russians bought into the mystique of the East.

What can we make of this westward urge? One practical suggestion is easy: if you plan to invest in land, buy west of the city. Beyond that, we can ponder endlessly how the "infinite West" has molded the American spirit. Americans have always been able to "go west" in spirit, if not always in fact, leaving behind disappointments and limitations. The West was a state of mind that allowed Americans to think big and live large. It was the root and the flower of the fabled American drive, idealism, and optimism that transformed the world.

For many Americans the ideal of the "infinite West" is closing. If it fades, what will it mean for America and the world?

Article 70:
Philosophic Fictions

German philosopher Martin Heidegger said that for no discernible reason or purpose man is "thrown" into the world where he must struggle to make sense of the mystery and misery of being. For Spanish thinker Ortega y Gasset, man is like a shipwrecked sailor who either sinks into the depths or swims toward an unseen shore that he may never reach. French philosopher Jean-Paul Sartre wrote that condemned to the forlorn freedom of abandonment, man must create his own essence and meaning in an absurd, uncaring world.

But if we think realistically about human life, we realize that these melancholy descriptions are philosophical fictions. The very term "man" is a linguistic convenience and an empty abstraction. To speak of man is to speak of men, and to speak of men is to speak of women, and to speak of both is by necessary implication to include family and society: boys and girls, the young and the old, and countless other people who in diverse ways and with varying intensity enter and exit our life. But even this realization leaves us on an abstract plane unless we can call these persons by name and tell something of their story.

A problem with philosophy is that it tends to be a solitary business lacking the correctives of other viewpoints. This is why philosophers often forget the mothers who bore and fed them, the fathers who protected and provided for them, the relatives, rivals, friends, neighbors, teachers, and lovers who shaped their lives and taught them almost everything they know about the world. Despite these realities, philosophers often give the impression that they are like the goddess Minerva, who sprang fully mature from the brain of Jupiter.

Living is primarily living with other people. This means that in a paradoxical way we experience solitude only because we are first of all social beings. If we were truly alone without the experience or memory of others, we would be unaware that we were alone, just as we would not think of ourselves as men or women without the other sex as a reference. Opposites may sometimes attract; they always identify.

Robinson Crusoe and similar cases of island castaways are commonly considered to be prototypical solitary humans. But even they were not without the human coexistence that made them aware of their solitude. Crusoe carried with him to the island a remembered culture that included language, religion and several technical skills. He had at his disposal weapons and tools from an advanced civilization, and more important, the ideals and beliefs of the society in which his humanity took shape.

The few documented cases of humans entirely deprived of human society are pathetic creatures lacking the linguistic skills that cannot exist apart from a living society. And without speech, human intelligence remains severely limited. It appears that everything truly human must be thought, taught and learned in a social context, including the melodramatic ruminations of philosophers.

Article 71: Our Preexistent Life

In his *Introduction to the Sciences of the Spirit* German philosopher Wilhelm Dilthey reminds us that human life does not begin—or end—at zero. Much of our life, perhaps most of it, must precede us in order for us to live humanly at all. This is not a reference to reincarnation or the preexistence of souls but to the pre-established world that shapes our life. According to an ancient proverb, "a man resembles his times more than he resembles his father." We can say then that our life becomes a dramatic tension between established canons—customs, religions, styles, beliefs, ideas—and the personal way we configure our life within them. This means that we are the artists or authors of ourselves who must dramatically shape life with preexisting colorings and components. To illustrate, countless unknown persons spoke our language into existence long before we born. But we give it our personal style and stamp, which then flows on as an infinitesimal part—in most cases—of the preexistent reality of unborn generations. What we call formal education is a veneer added to the immemorial knowledge we learn as children.

This continuing drama of life is not always apparent. In many persons the creative will is weak, giving the appearance of conformity to whatever befalls them. Ironically, it is the great rebels who show most forcefully how much the preformed world acts as the subsoil of our being. For rebelliousness can occur only within pre-established conformity. If there were no such expectations, there could be no rebellion against them.

This preexistent being before our personal being began gives human life an inescapable historical continuity. It is what philosopher Arthur Lovejoy called "the great chain of being" or in a more intimate way, thinker Miguel de Unamuno described as "intrahistory," that is, history played out at a daily, personal level.

Dilthey had a slippery intuition rather than a clear concept of human historicity. In 1883 he published the first volume of his *Introduction to the Sciences of the Spirit*. His announced second volume never appeared. Instead, for his remaining twenty-eight years he wrestled with ideas that were bigger than he was. The prevailing intellectual culture did not help. Hegel and Marx spread the notion that history alone does not explain itself but needs injections of abstract or economic reason to make it understandable. Dilthey struggled with the more radical idea that history is a deeper form of reason that shapes us. He could not overcome the popular ideas of his predecessors and his name is largely forgotten. But if his personal efforts were frustrated, his work did not end in vain. Later thinkers rediscovered his ideas and used them to enrich both historiography and philosophy. For instance, Spanish philosopher Ortega y Gasset gets credit for the celebrated statement, "Man does not have a nature, what he has is a history." The words are Ortega's, the idea is Dilthey's.

Article 72:
Our Better Half

At the most basic level, we can identify ourselves only by reference to the other sex. If there were no men, women would not know that they are women. And without women, men would not think of themselves as men. A verse by poet Antonio Machado sums it up nicely: "A man is not a man until he hears his name from the lips of a woman."

But this reference to the other gender means more than the man-woman disjunction. It also opens the way to personal fulfillment. The ancient Greeks believed that a man or a woman was only half of a whole person. The other half was missing, and according to Plato, when a person meets his or her other half they have an overpowering urge to unite and be complete. They see in each other the happy fulfillment of themselves. We still say a bit jokingly "my better half" in English, or in Spanish, *mi media naranja* (my other half of the orange). In English it always means the wife, but in reality the "better half" is either half, because ideally each is the fulfillment of the other.

Gender equality is one of the great causes of our time. But as important as it is, the relationship of the sexes goes far beyond legal equality and points to a dynamic, ever-moving balance of the sexes. Instead of a war of the sexes, think of it as a waltz in which each move by one partner corresponds to a matching maneuver by the other.

For this reason, it is impossible for one sex to change without a compensating change in the other. A dramatic shift in the aims and ambitions of women necessarily provokes corresponding alterations in male attitudes and behaviors. And so the dance continues. Not that the correlation is exact or centered on the same things. Men naturally admire women but often mistreat them, especially as they venture into areas once considered male strongholds. Men are still developing new attitudes for dealing with women as partners, competitors, and bosses.

The consequences can sometimes be negative. Some men react with hostility and unethical behavior to what they perceive as female intrusions into their turf. For their part, women may adopt coarse male vices in a misguided attempt to prove their equality.

But there are offsetting benefits for both sexes, among them a more dynamic and productive society. Alexis de Tocqueville noted that even with limited opportunities, energetic women deserved much credit for the vitality of early America. Today, their upward mobility also means more opportunities for what I call "sexuate friendships." I introduced the word "sexuate" in an earlier column. It refers to relationships in which gender is a conditioning factor but sexual liaisons are not. As one writer puts it, "In many cases, my best friends are women." He said it with admiration and respect. I second his opinion because I believe these friendships are the best foundation for lasting unions.

Article 73:
The Age of Ideas

The eighteenth-century Enlightenment, sometimes called the Age of Ideas, was centered in France but with outliers in all the Western nations. France had many enemies, but even its enemies admired French culture and considered it the gold standard of civilization. The Enlightenment set in motion many of the ideals the world still pursues: equality and freedom, elimination of aristocratic privileges, access to education and opportunity, overthrow of despotic monarchies, establishment of representative government, and disestablishment of religion. Despite this meaty agenda, it was also the last time intellectuals had a sense of humor and caricature. Most of them were ever ready to party and enjoy life. They were like brilliant children playing with the exciting new toys we call ideas. Unlike contemporary thinkers who usually work in solitude, the Enlightenment geniuses thought best in conversation and company.

Consequently, Enlightenment ideas preserve a vivaciousness rare in our day. But there is more to the story. The Age of Ideas was the ultimate successor to the Age of Belief, in which by definition ideas were uncommon. When beliefs predominate ideas are scarce, but when they are vigorous and plentiful, it indicates that traditional beliefs have weakened. As prevailing beliefs deteriorated in the late seventeenth and early eighteenth centuries, ideas sprang up on all sides and in every discipline, from agriculture and education to governance and law. Ideas as such became the rage. But one belief remained to tower above all the ideas of the era: a belief in ideas themselves. Today, ideas are cheap currency and everybody has them. But in the Enlightenment they were new and aesthetically dazzling, characterized by verbal brilliance and, often, an irreverence for traditional institutions and customs. The Monarchy, Church, and Aristocracy were favorite targets of the likes of Voltaire, Montesquieu, and Diderot. In different but also brilliant ways, Franklin, Jefferson, Gibbon, Hume, d'Holbach, and Jovellanos were stellar international representatives of the Enlightenment spirit.

But for all its brilliance, the Enlightenment also had its dark side. In France itself it ended in the murderous rage of revolution that destroyed many of the best French minds. Napoleonic imperial wars followed that bled the French military dry. And not until forty years later in the reign of Louis Phillipe—a restoration monarch—did the French begin to receive their basic rights.

France, though afterwards culturally revered, never regained its former power. Magnificent as a monarchy, eventually it took a lesser role as a republic. In contrast, the Enlightenment ideas that had mixed results in France were destined to triumph wholeheartedly in America.

The joyous Age of Ideas faded into the humorless nineteenth century with its ponderous philosophies, burgeoning sciences, and sprawling empires. With the end of Enlightenment gaiety a splendor had passed from the earth. No wonder French minister Tallyrand would reminisce many years later that those who had not lived in Paris around 1780 could not possibly know how good life could be.

Article 74:
The Fifth Generation

A new generation has appeared, but because it differs in form and function from its predecessors, we must summarize its history, not simply give it another cute label. This new generation is not the youngest, the subject of much notoriety, but the oldest, about which we hear little. Until the twentieth century people died at around sixty. Some lived longer, but like an army decimated in a ferocious battle, the survivors were too few and enfeebled to be a social force. Retirement systems such as Social Security still reflect actuarial tables based on the average life span of late nineteenth-century populations and the operative principle that to retire was to expire.

The vague notion of genealogical generations does not explain generational dynamics. The few available scientific studies of generations reveal that they overlap, like roof tiles, at roughly fifteen-year intervals, or levels. This means that at any given time in a sixty-year life span, four generations at different levels interact: childhood (0-15); youth and early adulthood (16-30); maturity and responsibility (31-45); seniority and dominance (46-60). There are also generational clusters—the Soviet experiment, for instance—structured around a dominant religious or ideological theme. In the short life spans of primitive humanity probably only two or three generations interacted.

The average American life span has increased to around eighty years. This increased longevity means that a fully populated and active fifth generation has joined the interactive mix. Several current presidential candidates belong to it. And a sixth generation seems to be forming as longevity increases.

If today young people take their time to grow up and assume responsibility, the elderly are in no hurry to die and relinquish it. Fifth-generation persons run corporations, control wealth, and wield political power at ages their ancestors never reached. This suggests an obverse relationship between extended youthfulness and elderly predominance. The young can avoid responsibility for running the world because mature generations do it for them. In earlier times extended youthfulness was not possible. At twenty-eight, Thomas Jefferson wrote the Declaration of Independence in a mature, majestic prose that we can barely associate with a person so young. The demographics of that period allowed no delays. People married early, lived quickly, and died soon.

Today, just as people devote more time to youthfulness, so others have many years of mature power and plenitude. But we should remember that in emergencies our "overage teenagers" may quickly stop their games and assume leadership. We do not really know people—ourselves included—until the test comes, and the transformation can be sudden and startling.

Increased longevity wreaks havoc with retirement schemes and health care. The long range effects are less obvious but probably even more drastic. By adding a new element to the generational chemistry, society becomes exponentially more dynamic and divisive as the intergenerational synapses increase. The days of placid, collective life appear to be over. But exactly how this five-dimensional complexity will affect life remains to be seen.

Article 75: Psychic Pollutions

For decades concerned organizations have crusaded against environmental pollution. Despite certain witless extremes, the cause is good. The purity of air, water, and food, and the responsible use of resources are necessary for our biological survival in this crowded world. And the concern is not for ourselves alone; as guardians of Nature, we feel morally responsible for the preservation and welfare of its creatures, and in the widest sense, of the earth itself.

But while insisting on clean air and water, we permit psychic pollutants to damage the core of our being. We allow vulgarities, obscenities, and unwholesome images that coarsen behaviors and dull sensitivities. It is not simply a matter of taste. Scientific studies on language acquisition, for instance, show that certain types of primitive music not only diminish intelligence but also pose health risks, just as music of a higher order enhances mind and body. Human life has a deep affinity for beauty and order.

There are worse pollutants. Our ideas and beliefs are the most intimate and personal level of our life. The truth they contain allows us to understand reality and live an authentic human life. Mountains of ideas and information are available to us. But just how many of them are false? How much of what we hear and see distorts reality and falsifies our life? How can we tell the difference between true voices and false echoes and adjust our direction accordingly? Perhaps the old idea of periodic examinations of conscience still applies in our time.

Often those who spread erroneous ideas are sincere people,

but sincerely wrong. The principle that a fool and his money are soon parted does not apply to the sincere person with a soapbox fidelity to a falsehood. Instead, it is likely that such a person will infect others who are equally susceptible. This is especially true in our day when both truth and falsehood come in a bewildering assortment of forms and from countless sources. But this much is certain: those addicted to falsehood will angrily resist corrective knowledge. From a teacher's perspective, better an empty mind than one filled with sophisticated but false ideas.

But beyond all these, deliberate lies are the most harmful psychic pollutants of all. Under a misguided sense of obligation, I wasted time before I realized that no good comes of attending conventions or agreeing to collaborations if the agenda is an affront to the truth. It is liberating to decide that insofar as possible we shall have no part in campaigns that disseminate lies. It is possible and even commendable to work with people whose intellectual gifts are modest, provided we may expect from them sincerity, truthfulness, and awareness of their limitations. For these are conditions we all share. But for those whose agenda is the psychic pollution we call lying, we should avoid them like the plague they are. Our silence may not be the perfect remedy, but it is still golden.

Article 76:
When Crime Was King

A skeptic could argue that civilization has been a never-ending struggle between those who make the laws and those who break them—in some cases the same people. Most of us think we are experiencing the greatest crime wave in American history. But we may be wrong. Earlier Americans were no slouches when it came to crime. Professor Cesare Lombroso, the father of criminology, said that the lawlessness that prevailed in America from the 1860's through the 1890's was "an American phenomenon with no equal in the rest of the world." Although statistics of that era may not be entirely accurate, they support his statement. During those decades it was reported that the crime rate rose 445 percent, while the population increased 170 percent.

The "Wild West" was blamed for much of the American lawlessness and condemned by one writer as "a great dismal swamp of civilization." But in that era New York City led the major urban centers of the world in crime. Slums were the primary breeding grounds for lawlessness, but both business and residential areas were infested with burglars, muggers, and murderers. As *Leslie's Weekly* commented in 1868, "We see ghastly records of crime. Murder seems to have run riot and each citizen asks, 'Who is safe?'" George Templeton Strong of the Gramercy Park area of New York noted in 1857:"Most of my friends are investing in revolvers and carry them about at night." He went on to say that "nocturnal fears of assault" were a city tradition.

But if New York led in crime due to its size, Chicago was

even worse statistically, and its criminals were tougher than their New York counterparts. According to police records of 1893, there was one arrest for every eleven residents, and though infinitely smaller than Paris, Chicago had eight times more murders.

Dark, poorly lighted streets added to the dangers, but muggings were common even in daytime. The rule in large cities was to avoid walking anywhere late at night. But if people had to go out, they were advised to go armed or with police escort. Otherwise, they were cautioned to walk in the middle of the street so that, as George Ade wrote, "no hold-up man could step from an alley and salute us with a piece of lead—or an elongated canvas bag filled with sand." New York's Central Park was even riskier than it is today.

The image of American lawlessness lingers. My foreign friends sometimes ask me how it is possible to live in this dangerous country. But people here ask me if I am afraid to go abroad. The irony is that just as foreigners are afraid of American criminality, so many Americans are fearful of other countries. I tell them that all countries are risky for the careless. As for me, I have been in many countries and—knock on wood—so far have fared well in all.

Article 77:
Ideas and Beliefs

Tell me what you believe and I will tell you that you are probably mistaken. Normally our real beliefs lie too deep for us to be consciously aware of them. They are like the subsoil under our feet. We do not hold beliefs; they hold us.

Beliefs are our unconscious assumptions of reality and have little to do with so-called "belief systems" that generate hatreds and loyalties. These are not beliefs but conscious ideas, customs, and opinions, or in more complex forms, ideologies.

The world we see before us is not reality itself but a structure that our unconscious beliefs superimpose on it. This is why when confronted with something that is completely outside our supportive beliefs we experience a visual and directional vertigo, as anyone who has ever been lost in a forest can tell you. We cannot see what our beliefs cannot first interpret.

When beliefs are strong ideas are scarce, and when ideas abound it is a sign that beliefs are weak. Ours is an era of weak beliefs, which explains the glut of ideas. Yet there is another connection between beliefs and ideas. Since the Enlightenment the Western nations have fed the world a rich diet of ideas in science, technology, entertainment, and political doctrine. Periodically these ideas march aggressively out of the West to conquer the rest of the world. All are impressive but not all are progressive.

These Western conquests are really more than conventional ideas. The highest achievement of the Enlightenment was the creation of a unique *belief in ideas*, that is, hybridized ideas with the force of unconscious belief but which exist at a conscious level.

In earlier times writers slavishly adhered to unquestioned authorities such as Aristotle or St. Thomas Aquinas. Personal ideas were considered unworthy, or worse, as sources of heresy. Voltaire, Rousseau, and other Enlightenment authors thrilled readers not only because of the radical ideas they espoused but also because they dared to flaunt their personal views. No wonder the United States was destined to excel as no other nation in this attitude. For it was the brainchild of the Enlightenment.

This belief in ideas was fun while it lasted. But now it is ending. Not that the number of ideas has decreased; on the contrary, we are awash in ideas, including the mass-produced versions cranked out by so-called "think-tanks." But ideas as such retain little of their former prestige and their very abundance is obverse proof that the belief on which they rest is losing its effectiveness.

If the Enlightenment belief in ideas has prevailed for over two hundred years, how do new beliefs replace them? There is a process, which cannot be rushed, by which ideas slowly evolve into new beliefs. The West has been creative as no other civilization in history. But it remains to be seen whether it can resolve with equal genius the most abused and misunderstood enigma of our time: the reality of the human person.

Article 78: Machiavellian Ethics

The age of great ideas and even greater ideals we call the Enlightenment culminated in the American and French Revolutions of 1776 and 1789, respectively. In both hemispheres it was the moment champions of the common people had long dreamed of. The Golden Age of humanity had arrived. Or so it seemed. A new era indeed had begun, but for all its glitter it was not quite golden.

The Americans soon consolidated their independence, but no sooner had the French delegates congregated in the National Assembly in 1791 than they divided according to political inclinations. Those who urged moderation and respect for civil order sat on the right. Those who advocated more draconian innovations took the left.

Thus began the rivalry of Left and Right. With many differences according to country and culture, it became the common political alignment of most Western democracies. The United States was long an exception. But in recent times the sharp Left-Right division has become the American political pattern as well.

Now, after more than two centuries, we ask, which side won? And the answer is, neither. A third contender for dominance, an older and more subtly crafted doctrine, degraded both Left and Right. It has a name and a profile. In modern times we call it Machiavellianism after Niccolo Machiavelli (1469-1527), whose book *The Prince* is a handbook of Machiavellian principles.

Machiavelli argued that a ruler may disregard traditional

ethics if deception serves the State. Of course there were unscrupulous rulers long before Machiavelli, but *The Prince* assured monarchs that they could be dishonest for sound reasons and with a clear conscience. The operative Machiavellian principle, what we may call the reverse ethics of Machiavellianism, is the use of low tricks to gain advantage. Evil is good if it leads to power, and good becomes evil if it hinders the process.

What began as a principle of statecraft soon infiltrated politics, business, and science. Left and Right resorted to unethical maneuvers with the Machiavellian argument that the end justifies the means, no matter how unsavory these may be. Commercial hyperbole brushed aside truth with the justification that "business is business," meaning that ethics must not stand in the way of profit.

At first, impersonal science seemed immune to such machinations. But starting with Leonardo da Vinci, scientists took sides and began designing instruments of war, By World War II scientific neutrality had become ethical indifference and political conformity. Far from being the hope of humanity, as earlier thinkers hoped, modern science is shared by the worst of enemies.

In the Machiavellian paradigm there is no punishment for wrongdoing provided one is sufficiently clever and ruthless. Instead, it seems to be a tempting shortcut to position and power. Yet as philosopher Jacques Maritain argues, the problems with Machiavellian reasoning reduce to one: its eventual and utter failure. Though unhurried in their verdict, history and human experience invariably prove him right.

Article 79: Roman Replay?

Can you believe that in a recent poll fifty-five percent of Parisians said they preferred to live elsewhere? For centuries Paris was the world's dream city, the capital of fashion, fine dining, art and culture. As an old song described it, "How ya gonna keep 'em down on the farm after they've seen Paree?" Will the new lyrics now be, "How ya gonna keep 'em back in Paree after they've seen the farm"?

Paris is not the first or only great capital agitated by dissatisfaction. Centuries before Rome fell, citizens were already moving to Mediterranean villas and distant lands like Provence and Iberia. Many patrician families left Rome so that the Roman legions could not conscript their sons. Others complained that undesirable immigrants—Germans, Jews, Christians, North Africans, and Mid-Easterners—threatened to overwhelm native Roman culture and religion.

Their fears were not unfounded. In 380 AD after prolonged persecutions to eradicate it, Christianity, once seen as another unwelcome Eastern cult, became the official religion of the Roman Empire under Theodosius. In 391, he shuttered all the old temples, leaving the traditional Roman gods Jupiter, Juno, and their cohorts to the *pagani*, or rural people. Our word "pagan" derives from the term, for country dwellers, as always, were the most conservative and the last to give up the old religion and convert to the new faith. But nothing saved Rome itself. By 800 AD it had shrunk from a city of over a million to a few hundred people living among the ruins and reminders of vanished glory.

We hear the cliché that America is going the way of Rome or that France may foreshadow our own national decline. But neither Imperial Rome nor centralized France matches the American paradigm. America does not stake its economic, cultural, and political destiny on a single great city like Rome or Paris, but distributes its energies in many states and cities in various stages of growth and vitality. When one declines, another rises to replace it. It took centuries for French kings to subdue the provinces and concentrate power in Paris. Americans resist the centralizing tendency and retain surprising vitality at state and regional levels. For example, most Europeans—and many Americans—do not realize that America has no national elections, only fifty state elections.

But perhaps the major difference is that in America the country and the city are not rigidly separated entities. Both are open, porous, and relatively free of mutual disdain. Rural America has taken its music, dress, and traditions into the city, and the city has brought its sports, food, and customs to the country. This symbiosis has blurred the lines and endowed both with a uniquely American brand of creative energy. We move easily in both realms—urbanized cowboys and ruralized city slickers.

What does it mean? Probably not all the old evils we fear to repeat but many good things we have yet to foresee.

Article 80: What Is Philosophy?

The short answer is almost everything and hardly anything. "Philosophy" is one those words like "complex" applied in recent decades to almost all kinds of clusters and combinations. Just as we speak of psychological, technological, or mathematical complexes, so it is common to use "philosophy" as a general synonym for almost any kind of strategy, for example, a "coaching philosophy" or an "investment philosophy."

The term is a combination of two Greek words, *philos* (love) and *sophos* (wisdom), and literally means a lover of wisdom. It was transliterated but never translated in the major Western languages. One philosopher described philosophy as "the general science of love." Other descriptions are much less poetic. Today we tend to think of philosophy in an academic sense as the teaching and study of a body of doctrines—metaphysics, ontology, epistemology, aesthetics, and several other dimensions—and because these studies are concentrated in universities, we think of philosophers, particularly in the United States and other English-speaking countries, as professors of philosophy. The identification is not false, but neither is it entirely true. Philosophy and philosophers are previous to these complexities and subdivisions.

In what way? Let us begin the simplification by pointing out what philosophy is not, at least not primarily. It is not a set of problems, nor a set of solutions, least of all, the intellectual manipulations of brainy people. It is not even primarily a matter of intellect but of outlook. There is an element of patience and respect in the philosophical mind which consists of allowing reality to display itself instead of imposing on it one's will and prior design. This means that above all philosophy is the art of seeing reality in its native, undistorted forms. Nothing is simpler to say or harder to do for most of us. Some people—artists for example—are born with the gift of perceptive seeing; others must learn to see through practice and persistence. For the latter, philosophy is a matter of "second sight," that is, learning to see again for the first time. What the philosopher must not do is close off the world and retreat into his/her own mind, which is the perennial temptation of the introverted thinker and the ruination of so many philosophies. The early Greek philosophers developed their thought not in secluded towers or quiet studies but in the noisy human traffic of the *agora*, or city square. What could be more fitting for the truly philosophical mind? What emerges is not, therefore, an unchanging set of doctrines but human responses to human problems. To say it in simpler words, philosophy consists not of its answers but its questions. This means that the prime philosophic imperative is to go on thinking and questioning. For when we see reality as it is we catch glimpses of the inexhaustible, astonishing richness of the Cosmos that moved the early Greeks to philosophize and set Western civilization on a path we still follow.

Article 81:
Tyrants and Totalitarians

When conditions became intolerable, ancient Greek cities would sometimes confer absolute but temporary power on a man they called a "tyrant." Like an Old West marshal, his task was to restore civil order and then resign. At first the title was benign and the office respected. It was not until some of the tyrants refused to give up their power that the term took on the derogatory meaning it has today. Likewise, the Romans could appoint a special magistrate called a "dictator" with the power to deal with emergencies. But like the Greek tyrants, the Roman dictators—Julius Caesar, for example—found ways to stay in power.

History is replete with tyrants, dictators, and despots. But in the twentieth century a new and more aggressive form of oppressive government appeared. It received a perfect name: *totalitarianism* because it sought total control over every aspect of life. In former times this scope of control would have been impossible. The state bureaucracy of the older despotic regimes was too weak and small, affecting only a few sectors such as religion, taxes, and the military. The bureaucracies of the modern democratic governments are far more efficient than the strongest tyrannies of the past. When Louis XIV supposedly made his famous statement: "I am the State," his boast was not far from the literal truth. It was beyond the capability of the old despotic rulers to control the economy or the private lives of people. They could dismiss ministers and lop off a few heads, but their power was limited. In the giant Spanish Empire, for instance, the monarchs decreed that native peoples were to be treated fairly and humanely and accorded full legal rights. But since most of the Spanish lands were largely self-governing and an ocean away, the rulers had no mechanism to enforce their decrees and prevent abuses.

In totalitarianism everything is relevant and under state control: economy, employment, family size, residency, language, education, religion, travel, and even thought. The advent of totalitarianism coincided with the rise of propaganda as an instrument of the Totalitarian State. In Hitler's time they called it the Big Lie. Truth is anything that serves the Totalitarian State; untruth, whatever works against it. This creates bizarre distortions: nonexistent democracies, make-believe elections, the fictitious sovereignty of enslaved peoples, and the massive paranoia of those to whom truth is an offense.

How do we explain these stifling totalitarian regimes in modern times when more people than ever are literate and living above subsistence levels? Perhaps Abraham Lincoln was right when he observed that what children learn in the classroom today they will apply publicly tomorrow. Many people scoffed at Nietzsche and Marx, but others used their ideas to bring misery to millions. If it is a matter of education, then maybe we should attach a warning label: *Danger. Education. Handle with care.*

Article 82:
A Look at Generations

To paraphrase what Mark Twain said about the weather, everybody talks about generations but nobody does anything about them. Well, that's not quite true; there are some exceptions. In Europe Karl Mannheim, Julius Peterson, Francois Mentre, Auguste Comte, Jose Ortega y Gasset, and Julian Marias have studied the generations.

Much less attention has been paid to the topic in English-speaking countries. Two exceptions are the translation of Marias' book *Generations: A Historical Method* (1970) and the collaborative book by William Strauss and Neil Howe, *Generations* (1991). In America, historians and social scientists—sticklers for precise documentation—seem to be as vague as the general public when it comes to a theoretical understanding of generations. But at least we give them catchy nicknames: Baby Boomers, Generation X, Millennials, etc. Yet the concept itself remains in a pre-theoretic stage with important questions unanswered. Is a generation simply a biological succession, as the Scriptures use the term? How long do generations last? What are the dynamics of their succession and overlapping? How and why is one generation different from another? How do they relate to history and society? Are generations apparent but not real?

Strauss and Howe tell us in vague terms that a generation is roughly twenty years long and marked by some important event in the early life of its members. American historian Theodore White suggests that generations occur in sixteen-year cycles as a function of presidential elections. Literary historians speak of "generations," a term for elite groups or schools of writers and poets. I had no confidence in any of these imprecise notions.

Still skeptical, I read Marias' summary of previous studies, including Ortega's theory. I admired Ortega for other ideas but not for his generations theory. According to him, a generational series starts with an outstanding person who supplies an organizing theme, which continues with diminishing force during a typical "epoch" of six fifteen-year generations. Normally, each succeeding generation has a decreasing level of loyalty to the master theme. But a predominant theme such as a religion or philosophy may repeat in successive renewals and declines.

Still a doubter, in 1984 I applied the theory as Marias refined it, using the Soviet Union as the target culture. The theory indicated major shifts at or near fifteen-year intervals— beginning close to 1915 (1917 was the actual start) with future markers around 1930, 1945, 1960, and 1975—and the likely end of the epoch around 1990. I was astonished years later when the Soviet collapse happened on schedule. A fluke? Maybe, and I remain skeptical. But this much seems clear: without a scientific theory of generations, they will remain a loose cannon, undermining assumptions and exposing some of the social sciences to charges of scientific softness.

Article 83: Insanity and Other Sayings

"The definition of insanity is doing the same thing over and over again and expecting different results." Albert Einstein usually gets credit for this popular saying. But it is doubtful that he coined the phrase or ever said it at all. At least when asked about it, he did not have a clear recollection of saying it. One version of the aphorism may go back to Benjamin Franklin, or perhaps to Mark Twain. It is the kind of insightful remark we would expect from these witty writers, especially the latter. Another possibility though, and maybe the most likely, is novelist Rita Mae Brown. The strongest argument for her authorship is the similar tone of her many irreverent but clever quips, including the following: "Morals are private, decency is public," and "If it weren't for the last minute, nothing would ever get done."

But regardless of who coined the saying, as it stands, it fails at least one test of logic. Obviously whoever said it never had to practice shooting free throws, tossing horseshoes, learning to play the piano, memorizing lines in a play or mastering Latin declensions. All of these require perseverance and countless repetitions, for practice makes perfect—to cite another time-worn cliché of unknown authorship.

The truth of both sayings may be jumbled up in a confusion of terms and the conditions they describe. Practice involves the perseverance necessary for the perfection of a skill or talent (though one must have the skill or talent to start with). But mindless repetition of the kind implied in the Einsteinian (?) definition of insanity is called "perseveration," a term usually confined to technical psychological language. It describes a compulsive, pathological repetition of an act or gesture. It is the opposite of progress toward perfection we associate with intelligent practice. Instead it is the kind of "running in place" that never goes anywhere.

Philosopher George Santayana authored at least three celebrated sayings, presented here in descending order of popularity: (1) "Those who cannot remember the past are doomed to repeat it"; (2) "Fanaticism consists of redoubling your effort when you have forgotten your aim"; and (3) "Only the dead have seen the end of war."

Many sayings are modern translations of Classical aphorisms: *Dum vita est, spes est* (Where there's life, there's hope). *Errare est humanum* (To err is human). Sayings once circulated throughout the European languages. Sometimes in rhyme to help people remember them: "Birds of a feather flock together"; (German) *Der frühe Vogel fängt den Wurm* (Equivalent: The early bird gets the worm): (French) *mieux vaut prévenir que guérir* (Equivalent: An ounce of prevention is worth a pound of cure).

Many of the older sayings have disappeared, along with the rural life on which they were based. Today we are more likely to quote movie stars or popular writers. As the ancients said, *Omnia mutant*—all things change.

Article 84:
The Sounds of Silence

Now and then I return to the ruins of a little house my Great Grandfather built in lower Appalachia in the 1800s. It is about as far as you can get from power lines, signal towers, airports, and paved roads. The forest—eternal enemy of human creations—has recaptured the homestead with second-growth trees: mostly pines, sassafras, and scrubs instead of hickories and oaks. The old wagon road disappeared long ago and unless you know the location, you might never find the place.

There is not much left: the collapsed sandstone chimney—"chimley" in hill country speech—a few of the sturdier foundation beams, and, above all, a lingering nostalgia. The latter distorts any rational assessment of what was once there, which was never much to start with. Great Grandfather and his mountain neighbors were poor people, not by comparison with wealthier folk, for there were none, but in what we consider essentials: electricity, radio, television, telephones, groceries, schools, books (exception: a Bible), doctors, and running water. We have many more needs than they did. The very thought of indoor toilets would have sounded indecent to them. I have never found any sign of a well, so I think they must have carried water from the creek two hundred yards from the house.

But if their world was poor in things, it was rich in silence. If other people are with me, I ask them to shut down their phones, pads, music, and chatter, and for ten minutes at least to listen again to the silent world of our ancestors.

The effect is eerie. Real silence is not silent but filled with messages just beyond the range of hearing. We never understand them, but in some way they understand us. After a time, our heart rate slows, mental clutter subsides, and the world returns to its ancient hierarchy. It is not that earlier people were deaf to sounds. On the contrary, a barking hound, squawking chickens, or the cries of forest animals and birds alerted them to events and dangers we do not notice today.

A human voice could elate them. Company was the highest form of entertainment. And voices were not divorced from human faces. People of Great Grandfather's time peered intently at people's faces, reading them to detect nuances, lies, and truths that went beyond words. I remember some of the old ones whose penetrating stares could be unnerving. This is why earlier generations disliked telephones, which separated people from their voices. And if they were illiterate, as many of them were, their memory compensated; they remembered nearly everything they heard. Once they met you, they never forgot your name, family affiliation, and other facts about you. In a world of few people, human reality was supreme.

They were unimaginably tough by our standards. They watched their children die in childbirth or childhood, dug their graves, prayed for their souls, and returned to their labors. Great Grandfather lived into his nineties but Great Grandmother died early, done in by unassisted childbirth and crushing drudgery, like so many women of earlier times.

Great Grandfather's house and his world are gone forever. But it is good to remember that some of the things that vanished were worthy and some that replaced them are still questionable. I miss the humanized quality of life. This is why I go back now and then to listen to the restorative sounds of silence.

Article 85: Provincialism of the Powerful

A hundred years ago, Germany was the leading country in science and philosophy, while neighboring France was the world's literary and cultural center. Thomas Jefferson—some say Benjamin Franklin—verbalized a popular sentiment of earlier times: "every man has two countries, his own and then France." Fast forward a century and several wars and we find a much altered world paradigm. France and Germany are still respected powers, but today the United States is the leader in scientific research, innovative technology, and popular culture. As a result, English has replaced French as the international language of business, entertainment, and science. And millions of immigrants to the US have left the land of their birth for the land of their preference.

Yet all these leading nations share, or have shared, at least one negative feature. I call it the "provincialism of the powerful" and define it as general indifference toward anything beyond their borders. Today, in order to be credible, scientists and intellectuals of all countries must know English, just as their predecessors once had to know French and perhaps German before World War I. On the other hand, many English-speaking intellectuals and researchers do not learn other languages and thus do not know—or care—much about other cultures. They assume that anything worth knowing is already available in English. This is true of current science, at least the so-called "hard" sciences, but not of philosophy and literature, areas in which translation is often extraordinarily difficult and professionally not highly regarded or remunerative.

In the early years of the twentieth century well-read young scholars from other countries who traveled to Germany and France were astonished to learn that in some cases illustrious intellectuals of these nations knew little about what was going on next door. This was partly due to the historical enmity between France and Germany, but the stronger reason was the conviction that their respective cultures were too advanced for them to bother with any other.

Today, intellectuals in other countries are obliged to keep up with just about everything that happens in America, as they did with France and Germany in their heyday. But there is at least one important difference: Americans must have some awareness of other cultures not because they esteem the culture itself but for political, economic, or military reasons. Otherwise, the conventional pattern of earlier predominant cultures prevails. Cultural preeminence tends to supersede individual talent, and secondary intellectuals, artists, and writers in American culture are favored over first-rate figures in less prominent countries. This "provincialism of the powerful," the belief that nothing worthy can come from the Galilees of the world, continues to be a paradoxical weakness common to great cultures, including our own. It is a creature of cultural pride. But pride limits us, for as sages have always taught, it is particularly susceptible to blindness and prone to falling.

Article 86: Facial Philosophy

The philosophy of the human body is still in its infancy, but we know enough to agree with Abraham Lincoln that after about age forty we are responsible for our face. Living is a frontal task: we face the future and the consequences are imprinted on our face and limned in our eyes. Behind our inherited ancestral features, our face reveals how we have fared in life. Our wins and losses mark it; loves and hatreds mold it. It tells our personal tale of delights and regrets.

Prosopon and *persona*, Greek and Latin terms, respectively, originally meant "face," but later also referred to the tragic or comic masks actors wore to hide their faces. In contemporary English, "persona" is an outer personality that covers the inner person. Ironically, the face, which reveals the most about us, may also conceal the most.

A feminine face activates its own set of expectations in us. Ideally we hope to see beauty in the female face, or the grace that suggests it, and experience a brief disappointment when neither is present. Woman is usually lighter of body and facial features than man and less exposed to the harsh forces that harden his life and features. Her charm draws him out of the masculine silence that settles over many men with maturity. She frees him to be young and verbal again. Ever the extremist, man may outdo her: if she is crude, he may sink to depravity; if talkative, he may turn lyrical. Plato said that when love is in the air, man turns poetic.

What do we see in a masculine face? Not the same charm that graces the feminine countenance. For this reason, many languages, including English, have different words to indicate feminine beauty and male handsomeness. Womanly beauty in a male face is disturbing, and we hardly know what to make of it. Unless the male face reveals a frivolous life—human life admits of degrees—we expect to see seriousness, what the Romans called *gravitas*. It corresponds to grace in woman. Man is solidly planted, and it usually takes woman's effervescent charm to rapture him out his heavy responsibilities and turn his life toward happiness.

But there is another side to man's being. With his feet on the ground and the world on his shoulders—every responsible man is to some degree an Atlas—he often feels a strange wanderlust. He is planted here but he dreams of elsewhere, of far lands and distant shores. Traditionally, woman incites him to pursue her, but she runs only so far before the urge to settle into domesticity prevails. Then she fears that he may not stop when she does, that her charms will not hold him to marriage and family. This is why woman often fears man's greater ambitions and urges compromise and security over risky achievement. But since men and women seem to be converging in their behaviors in recent decades, both sexes now share this fear.

Article 87:
Noble Obligations

The spread of human rights and freedoms is arguably the most impressive feature of modern democratic societies. Since tyrants always lose the ideological battle with the democratic ideal, they are forced into the dictatorial hypocrisy of pretending to offer their people the same rights they trample. The victimized people are cowed but not deceived. Democracy is everywhere the winner, shining by example where it exists or by its absence where prohibited.

The very success of the modern drive to extend rights and freedoms to all people encourages us to see the State as the fail-safe guarantor of human rights. But just as nothing human is foolproof, so the State is not immortal. It may mutate into something quite different or collapse completely. Democratic Germany voted Hitler into power, who then abolished democracy and voting altogether. When the Roman Empire collapsed so did Roman citizenship and the legal rights it offered.

You may be readying objections to a comparison with human rights in American society. You may point out that the American experiment with democracy took a Christian tack and that the Creator, not human government, was the Author of human rights. But modern governments, including our own, are now thoroughly secularized, which could mean that our ship of State is no more seaworthy than the Roman version that sank ages ago.

All this is prologue to the main point. It has to do primarily not with one's rights but with one's obligations, not with what government can confer on us—and as readily take away—but what we can do on our own. I refer to the inner code by which some people rise above the common rut of life and require of themselves more than they ask of others. In earlier times it was called *noblesse oblige*, "nobility obliges," a survival of the old chivalric spirit evident in all kinds and conditions of people. We hear that chivalry is dead, but if so, its ghost is still active. It consists of defending the defenseless, respecting all people, remaining faithful to truth, and serving those too poor or weak to serve themselves.

Not that this attitude toward life necessarily leads on to fame and accolades. This was the dream and downfall of Don Quixote. Instead it means asking oneself the best way to proceed with any task or act. For there is always a better or worse way to do anything.

In reality, it amounts to a deeper decision to become a better or worse person than we have been. It is both repentance and renewal of life. For human life, unlike any other reality we know of, allows the thrilling but perilous possibility of becoming more or less than we have been. *Noblesse oblige*, nobility obliges, not by formal or inherited right but by a personal code of conduct and conviction. It is not the story of a famous few but an option available to all.

It is, I believe, the ultimate human right.

Article 88: Speedy Americans

Americans have always been in a hurry. In an 1872 New York traffic report there is a description of carriages, stagecoaches, cartmen, and pedestrians ". . . all melted together in one agglomerate mess" and all ". . . seemed driven by some frantic demon of haste." But New York was only one of many places afflicted with speed demons. Burgeoning Chicago was another. In <u>The Texan Immigrant</u> (1840) Colonel Edward Stiff described Houston as a city where impatient, short-tempered people of every coloring and culture rushed through the muddy streets bent on making their fortune—or taking someone else's. Road rage is nothing new; Stiff tells of frequent fights over road slights. Many Houstonians scoffed at what little law there was. Stiff's landlady not only stole his possessions but also dared him to do something about it.

Many European visitors to the United States were shocked by American haste and informality. They ate in a hurry so as to get back to work. German Frederick Gustorf wrote that Americans did not know how to relax and enjoy life. Business was the only pleasure they knew. Taking a parting shot at "ugly' American women, he returned to Germany in high dudgeon.

Unlike Gustorf, Alexander Farkas approved of the American "lack of surface veneer." President Andrew Jackson treated him with warmth and informality, prompting the astonished Farkas to remark that one almost forgot that Jackson was President of the American Republic of 13 million people. But Farkas agreed with Gustorf that the driving force in American life was the acquisition of wealth.

American energy has never diminished. In Montreal I once asked a European philosopher what difference he saw between American and Canadian cities, otherwise so similar in appearance. Without hesitation he said, "It's a difference of movement. American cities have a higher level of energy and activity."

Like all adolescents, America was in a hurry to grow up. It rushed through the stages of development. Whereas it took Europe centuries to plod through the Middle Ages, Renaissance, Reformation, Enlightenment, and Modernity, the United States raced through shorter but similar stages. For example, the fiercely independent cattle barons of the American West were cut from the same mold as the rough European barons who defied kings when necessary to defend their lands and privileges.

But not everything in America was hasty. Even as European serfdom—a milder slavery—was disappearing, it was resurrected in a harsher form in Southern plantation society, itself a rebirth of medieval English manorial life. Its unhurried pace and rigid class structure were strangely at odds with the rest of informal, hurried America. The South was "old" not only in time but also in form. More than a purely American phenomenon, it was a survival of an older, slower society. The Old South was the medieval world's last bastion and the Civil War its last stand against modernity. Born in old Europe, it died in young America.

Article 89: Sexual or "Sexuate"?

One of the first things we learn as babies is that there are two kinds of people, the large beings called men and women, or in their younger and smaller versions, boys and girls. With this knowledge soon comes the realization that we belong to one or the other group and that each has its set of expectations and prohibitions. Mothers dress baby girls in pink, boys usually in blue. Parents pick names from a socially approved list for girls and from another for boys. Only a few names can apply to either gender, and it is generally considered to be unfair, if not cruel, to saddle a child with a name usually reserved for the other sex.

As they grow up, children learn that there are gender-appropriate toys, games, and clothing. Although rigid distinctions have softened considerably in recent decades, they have not yet disappeared entirely. This flexibility has favored women and girls, giving them entry into erstwhile male domains, particularly dress codes, behaviors, and professions. Today, with full respectability women can dress like men and swear like sailors, but society still regards men who wear feminine apparel as comical caricatures.

All this and heightened political sensitivities to gender in Western societies would have us believe that we are immersed in a sexual world. But even though sex is the general innuendo of our time, the language we use to verbalize these concepts turns out to be surprisingly defective. Since the advent of Freudianism, the underlying thought about our relationships with the other gender is that they are openly or subliminally sexual. But the truth is that strictly sexual relationships are statistically rare. The vast majority of our dealings with the other sex have nothing to do with sexual intentions or acts. But if not sexual, then how do we describe them?

While translating a book years ago on relationships between the sexes I came across the word *sexuado*, itself a neologism, or invented word, coined by Spanish philosopher Julian Marias. Lacking an equivalent in English—"sexist" and "sexed" were already degraded—I recast the word as "sexuate." Sexuate relationships exist between celibate persons, the young or elderly, siblings, parents, children, and the vast majority of people of the other sex.

But there is an even more important sexuate relationship in marriage. Sexual attractions are intense but they tend to be episodic and often short-lived, as they are in nature. This is why without sexuate friendship, marriages and similar unions based on sexual attraction alone tend to end quickly in divorce or separation—the familiar Hollywood pattern—or to linger as one of humanity's greatest miseries. But for those whose marriage and sexual intimacy occur within a context of sexuate friendship, which either preceded the union or developed soon thereafter, marriage can be one of life's happiest experiences. Millions of people could testify either way.

Article 90: The Art of Being Human

Historian Thomas Carlyle (1795-1881) made the celebrated statement that history does not reveal its alternatives. His observation was compatible with several prevalent philosophies of that era—Positivism, Marxism, Naturalism—all of which shared the common feature of explaining human behavior in terms of scientific forces: natural phenomena, economic theory, evolutionary biology, etc.

The problem was, and remains, that no matter how trivial human life may appear to be, it is a unique category irreducible to secondary or abstract features. Economic, biological, sociological and similar influences are important, but the primacy of life cannot be explained by its secondary features. On the contrary, the overreaching feature of human life is our inherent personal freedom, which has frustrated so many theoreticians of the abstract and defeated a multitude of totalitarian despots. Someone has said that the first exception to the Marxist theory of economic determinism was Karl Marx himself. As existential philosopher J.P. Sartre put it, man is necessarily free, whether he wishes to be or not. This means that life is not given to us as a finished commodity designed by abstract principles, but comes into being only as we live, only as we choose, reject, justify, love, detest, confront—and even create—our alternatives. Nor can we overlook the rectification of life we call repentance, not possible in any other reality we know of. Generally we think of it in a religious context, but it applies as readily to the whole of life. We always have the freedom to change course. This is why in order to understand anything human we cannot cite a theory but must offer a narrative. The ancient Greeks wisely refrained from honoring or vilifying those still living, for they knew not how their lives might turn at last to good or evil. For this reason, human life, personal or historical, is inherently dramatic, a quality that pertains only slightly, if at all, to other realities. It is the difference between living and existing. We know from the start the existence of a stone but cannot foretell how a living person or a people will develop or regress. This why every life is a novel, and why also human history not only reveals its alternatives but in time may become them.

The modern habit of seeing people through economic, political, or other lenses seems to be associated with a general lowering of international esteem. Today hardly any nation admires any other. If in earlier times nations were extolled for their human merits, today we tend to scorn them for their economic deficiencies. Ancient Greece and biblical Israel were small, resource-poor nations to which modern people would not give a second look. As far as we know, Moses and the prophets worked without salary, and Socrates and the philosophers dealt in the intangible currency of ideas. But what they taught the world became the enduring legacy of Western civilization: the art of being human.

Article 91: The Generosity Principle

The generosity principle, sometimes called the charity principle, is a method of overcoming rival arguments by first acknowledging their truth, or at least the reasons why people believe them to be true. Despite this commendable openness to reality, however, it usually loses out to ad hominem arguments that consist of attacking the messenger instead of the message. Ad hominem tactics work in politics but will get you a failing grade in logic 101.

To step away from the heat of today's political squabbles, consider the classic rivalry between capitalism and communism. A century of ad hominem arguments and very little generosity has made both terms hateful to the opposing camps. To the capitalists, communism is a metaphor for political tyranny and economic ruination, and with equal disdain, the communists look on capitalism as the epitome of worker exploitation and class inequality. As heirs of the capitalist world, how should we deal with the communist point of view?

To begin with, we admit that indeed nineteenth-century capitalism was often abusive. Workers were essentially at the mercy and whim of employers. Working conditions were deplorable, for instance, in London where Karl Marx and Friedrich Engels published their Communist Manifesto in 1848, and no better in New York crammed to overflowing with thousands of immigrant workers. Employers had the exclusive power to set wages, working hours and conditions, and workers had no right to appeal any of them.

But Marx did not, and could not, tell the whole story. The

picture he painted of capitalism was frozen in a moment of time and did not include subsequent improvements in the form of labor unions, better wages, arbitration boards, humane working conditions, health care, and the right to strike. The gruesome picture of early capitalism remained and became an enduring stereotype of worker exploitation. I used to hear this archaic view of capitalism from Marxist professors in Europe. Their indignation was genuine, but it was at least a century out of date. The American Marxists I knew had their causes and griefs, but primitive worker exploitation was not one of them.

All these improvements allowed capitalism to steal a march on their communist adversaries. While Marxism was stuck in old paradigms, pressing for basic worker rights already earned decades earlier, the West was achieving standards of living without precedent in human history.

But therein lay several problems. Western prosperity was not uniform; many populations were left behind. When everyone is poor, nobody thinks of themselves as poor. Prosperity defines poverty. Nothing is more dehumanizing than to be poor in a world where prosperity is perceived as a human right.

This brings up a second Marxist accusation. Communists see wealth as finite, which means that the rich nations must have robbed the poor ones. It is a logical but flawed assumption. Marxists limp along with this limited concept, but the world is more generous than they know and allows people of vision to create unlimited wealth.

Article 91:
The Disappearing Present

The Egyptian pyramids of Giza are immensely old, yet they are still the latest word in pyramids. In contrast, they tell me my three-year-old cell phone is already obsolete and ready for replacement. The Sphinx dates from around 2,500 B.C., but as sphinxes go, it is newer than my 2006 relic computer. Is there anything more obsolete than a newspaper from 1980, or more irrelevant than Super Bowl XXV? The minute we drive our new automobile off the dealer lot it starts to age almost as quickly as ice cream melting in a Texas summer.

On the other hand, going through some old family wills recently, I was struck by the way possessions once held their value over several generations. Clothing, especially overcoats, silks, and other finery, were passed on as valuable commodities. Pots, pans, plates, dishes, knives, forks, spoons, cups, beds, quilts, linens, furniture, implements, and utensils were carefully inventoried and distributed among heirs. Unlike our modern automobiles that quickly age into antiques, the same carriages, surreys, buggies, coaches, wagons, saddles, and harness served several generations. Horses, cows, and other animals died of course, but their replacements were replicas of others unchanged for thousands of years. All this had a way of prolonging the human present.

At the other extreme, philosopher Bertrand Russell argued that there is no such thing as the present time. An abstract line divides past and future time, and no sooner does it pass than the future is now the past without any real time in between. But this is an abstract and erroneous way of looking at time. What we call "our time" includes a fluctuating amount of the recent past and a variable segment of the future, which we claim as ours. In this sense, what we call "the present time" was once a much broader span of time in which obsolescence occurred much more slowly than it does today.

Today we crowd impatiently at the verge of the future and quickly abandon the past to the trash bin of history. From one week to the next few of us remember or care about former heroics or tragedies. The result is a narrowing of the temporal band we call the present. It is as though we were standing on a sandbar quickly dissolving under our feet. The clock and calendar, not intrinsic value, determine what deserves our attention. Publishing houses, automobile makers, and other manufacturers fudge on their production dates, stealing as much of the future as they dare to ward off disqualifying obsolescence.

Time is always short, which is usually a sign that we have misused it. In our race to be up to date on the latest, we eventually discover that we are, sadly, merely dated and late, having forfeited the fullness of present time, the primary condition of a full life.

Article 92: Propaganda

Propaganda, from Latin *propagare*—to propagate or spread—is one of those words in English that have declined in prestige but grown in popularity. It began as an ecclesiastical term referring to the propagation of Christian doctrine. But as the word spread to other languages, it took on the broader, but still innocent, meaning of promoting other kinds of doctrines. There it stopped in several of the Romance Languages and with minor spelling tweaks remains their word for commercial advertising—French *propagande*, Spanish and Portuguese *propaganda*.

In English the same word slid further down the scale, taking on a derogatory meaning especially in World War II with Hitler's use of the "Big Lie" and the later Cold War tendency of totalitarian states to call themselves "democratic republics" and gut words of their traditional meanings.

Americans opposed the practice but got used to the idea and put it to work in other ways. In the post-war economic expansion an explosion—hyperbolically speaking—of inflated advertisements replaced the staid promotions of pre-war America. No longer was it enough for products simply to be good and dependable; now they must be "fantastic" and "revolutionary." A car could not be merely a standard or deluxe model; now it must offer today futuristic engineering. Athletes, actors, and musicians were no longer stars; now either they were superstars or they were nothing. Today promotors hawk unexceptional films and books by describing them as "epic," "must-see," or "must-read." Probably nobody outdoes the pharmaceutical industry in exaggerating the benefits of its unpronounceable new drugs. The lame walk again, the breathless breathe, and the elderly know anew the pleasures of youth. But manufacturers are forced to make disturbing disclaimers: one drug may destroy your liver, another can give you a stroke, and a third may kill you. Minor inconveniences compared to the wonders they promise

Not only do we exaggerate praise; we go to similar extremes in criticism. Political or business rivals do not simply disagree; they "blast" or "destroy" one another. The language of invective has about it a roar of war and destruction, and often a few rounds of profanity for good measure.

Hyperbole is the new normal and we have worn out our superlatives trying to achieve it. We are surrounded by propaganda, or to use a cruder word, by lies. But these are consensual fictions. Like the proverbial frog unaware that the water he sits in is beginning to boil, we have grown used to lies and sense nothing amiss and demand nothing different. We may complain when a wheel falls off our uber-modern automobile, but we would be puzzled and maybe disillusioned if the manufacturers and promoters simply told us the plain truth, warts and all. What would be the fun and expectation in that? Ours has become a world of false echoes, but it entertains us with noise and gregariousness. Truth usually lies in a quieter direction, on a road that often we must walk alone.

Article 93: Originality

In my years as a book editor, I saw the strain writers were under to come up with original plots and characters. Most failed, but occasionally an author would succeed and a flood of "me-too" manuscripts would come across my desk. Most were rejected, but the process reminded me that what we understand by "originality" has at least two meanings.

Today we often try to be creative by being bizarre. But so is everybody else with the same hope, and we end up running with a herd. Anyway, twenty years or so from now, nearly everything we do today, the clothes we wear, the cars we drive, the music we listen to, the ideas we have, even our language, will prove to new generations that we were laughably cartoonish products of our time. The calendar eventually dooms us all to ridicule, which is a good argument against taking ourselves too seriously.

Medieval people had a radically different idea of originality, and consequently of literature. It was based on respect for changeless authority and tradition. Take Geoffrey Chaucer (1343-1400), the first great writer of the English language, as an example. If he wrote today, two Italian writers might sue him for plagiarism. Several of his *Canterbury Tales*—the *Knight's Tale*, for instance—closely resemble stories from the earlier *Decameron*, a collection of stories by Giovanni Boccaccio (1313-1375), and his *Troilus and Criseyde* is similar to themes found in the writings of both Boccaccio and Francesco Petrarch (1304-1374).

But the fact that Chaucer and others were honored for their

imitative writings tells us much about how people viewed literature in medieval times. Like children today, they wanted to hear the same familiar stories over and over. And the emphasis is on "hear" because very few people could read. The concept of plagiarism, or literary larceny, did not exist. Neither did copyright laws. Writers reworked traditional stories that were the cultural patrimony of all Europeans. Three centuries later, Shakespeare was still doing the same thing.

Medieval serfs seldom strayed from their manors, but at intellectual levels, medieval Europe was more international than in modern times. Nationalism was weak and boundaries porous. Latin was the universal European language of theology, law, science, and philosophy, which allowed professors and students to wander at will over Europe to lecture and study at great universities such as Oxford, Paris, Salamanca, Bologna, and Coimbra. These scholars were not searching for new theories but better renderings of authoritative knowledge. The quest for new knowledge was not a feature of universities until after the Copernican Revolution.

If asked, I tell writers what I finally discovered for myself. Originality happens when we are true to our origins. This does not mean limitation, much less imitation, but consists instead of a lifelong effort to elevate our own perspective to its plenitude. We may enrich it with additions, but we can never be really creative if we go through life trying to copy, in Shakespeare's words, "this man's art and that man's scope."

Article 94: The Faces of Janus

Janus was a two-faced Roman god for whom January was named. One face looked to the future, the other, to the past. It is a convenient metaphor for America, which also looks in both directions.

Primitive things have always charmed Americans. Although the "noble savage" undefiled by civilization was an ideal created by Rousseau and the European Romantics, it harmonized with American fascination with unspoiled nature and the Jeffersonian emphasis on human freedom, dignity, and equality. As civilization advanced and the image of the admirable savage faded, the Jacksonian ideal of the "common man" replaced it. Everything was done in his name, even if it was often taken in vain and without his participation.

A much older past also claims our attention. We give it impressive names that cover huge gaps in our knowledge: proto-history, Paleolithic or Neolithic ages, and beyond humanity itself, paleontology, paleozoology, and unimaginably long geological eras. Unlike the "noble savage" and "common man" once featured as literary and political themes, prehistoric humans or proto-humanoids are scientific icons. Instead of focusing on modern people in order to understand mankind, several scientific communities concentrate either on the remains of people dead for thousands of years or their vanishing counterparts who have existed for millennia in cultural time warps. The dead take precedence over the living. Neanderthals are more interesting than New Yorkers.

Our escapist desire to run away from the present is coupled

with this fascination with the past. And why not? If the key to humanity lies in ancient nature, what better way to rediscover ourselves than to return to it? The problem is that nature does not explain humanity, at least not what humanity has become. Nature is the limited world of the possible; technology allows us to enter the world of things that are naturally impossible. Today we do not merely walk, run, and talk to people nearby, but speed, soar, and speak across oceans.

We have another fascination, as Janus has another face. From our reverence for nature and the past we swivel to an escapist, spurious notion of the future. Philosopher Alvin Toffler called it "future shock," the title of his book. We can describe it as the aggressive tendency of the future to disqualify the present and declare it boring and out of date before it happens. It is the future that will not wait its turn and the present we cannot wait to be rid of.

Yet the future depends on our fidelity to the present, and so does fulfillment of the past. We are the future of those who lived before us and the past of those who will follow us. It is a dangerous temptation to declare our time unworthy of earnest commitment. With all its troubles, today is still worth the trouble; to dismiss it is to damage tomorrow. Like Janus, we must look back and ahead but always with a responsible vision of the here and now.

Article 95: The Problem with Critical Thinking

One of the mantras in our colleges and universities—and maybe in advanced high school classes, too—is that we must teach students to think critically. It sounds like solid pedagogical theory with roots in the ancient Socratic Method. Students need to be insightful, able to separate gold from glitter and truth from appearances. Above all, they should be able to give cogent reasons for their views. But in my experience and from what other professors tell me, it seldom works out that way. And once we ask some Socratic questions ourselves, we begin to see why it doesn't.

Two questions are fundamental: first, does the student have sufficient knowledge about the topic to be able to draw responsible critical conclusions, and, second, does the teacher have the ability, patience, and will to teach the critical methodology? Socratically, this would bring up a dialectical string of questions. But even if the eventual answer is yes, we are still in danger of violating one of the first rules of good pedagogy, which is to encourage in the student an attitude of enthusiasm for the material. Many students in our day are distrustful to begin with. We do them no favor by encouraging them to become even more sophisticated in their skepticism. Furthermore, it is usually academically fatal for the teacher to express what the students may take to be negativity about the subject, and almost anything that smells of criticism in the early stages of learning will be mistaken for it.

Often we put the academic cart before the pedagogical horse and ask students to evaluate what they have not yet learned. Unhappily, students tend to mistake the critical approach for a mandate to deconstruct—a softer word for destroy—the material instead of learning it.

There is a notion afoot in higher education that we can create knowledge simply by talking about it, often in small groups, which is the structure of first resort for many teachers, but one of the unholiest of academic creations unless the participants are advanced and committed to the topic. Otherwise small-group discussions in school, church, or business, usually degenerate into mechanisms for wasting time, telling war stories, and exchanging ignorance.

A time comes in the progression of serious students when they must "kill the Master," a harsh way of saying they must leave the mentor behind. Good teachers are the salt of the earth, but at a certain point students must wave goodbye to them and perhaps discard portions of what they have been taught. They could not have gotten this far without their teachers, but neither can they go further with them. Here the teacher can only point the way and step aside. From now on students must go it alone, doing for themselves what no teacher can do for them, which is the creative transformation of abstract lessons into personal knowledge. Only at this level can thinking become truly critical.

Article 96: The Naked Truth

Why people wear clothes is a question as old as humanity. We read in *Genesis* that because of their transgression the Edenic couple became aware of their nudity and in shame tried to cover themselves.

Three reasons given for wearing clothing are modesty, protection, and aesthetic enhancement. But this neat paradigm wobbles when we realize that some tribes go about totally or nearly nude. Nudity is understandable in the tropics, impractical in colder climates, and unfathomable in the case of early Patagonians who endured Antarctic winters almost completely nude. Clothing varies in cultures within the same climate zones. The African Tuaregs dress in long robes and turbans for protection against heat, but people in lower Africa wear hardly anything at all for the same reason. Classical Greeks admired the male figure—less so the female—and nude male athletes appeared not only in art but strolled about in public.

Taboos about nudity usually do not apply to infants. Their paradisiacal innocence removes any shame of their nudity. We envy babies their freedom from self-consciousness and adore them for their primal perfection. But it is an embarrassing invasion of privacy to walk in on nude adults, particularly the elderly.

Philosopher Martin Heidegger believed that clothing responded to the obverse human urges to conceal and reveal. But this begs the question by posing a deeper one: what do humans have to conceal or reveal in the first place? Current science likens humans to animals by ignoring their defining difference. An animal is what you see, but much of human life consists of what you do not see. For unlike animals, human reality possesses depth with secrets, passions, and yearnings too private and delicate for casual exposure. And the greater the depth, the deeper the humanity. This hints, but does not prove, that clothing is a means of subordinating the human animal to the human person.

To animals, Nature is a cruel mother, to humans, a tyrant. In neither case is she loving. To animals she makes no promise of survival and shows no grief when they die. Her best gift to them is instinct. But ages ago humans swapped instinct for intelligence, which meant that from then on, they would not conform to nature but would oblige nature to conform to them. The greatest advance of the creature Desmond Morris called "The Naked Ape" was not in physical changes—opposable thumbs, upright stance, furless bodies, etc.—but in the development of a psychic life of self-awareness, perception, reason and foresight. From now on humans would be shaped by concepts, ideals, and visions of things yet to be.

It is probably no coincidence that poetry of ideal love and beauty flourishes when people dress to the nines. Nudity in art may be admirable, but in the flesh it always disappoints because it leaves nothing to the imagination. And Einstein, who knew a thing or two himself, said that imagination is more important than knowledge.

Article 97: Miracle Fatigue

We live in an age of the impossible, or better said, an age in which the impossible has become routine. As I write this, there are human artifacts on the Moon, Mars, and a distant comet. Others hurtle through space headed for regions beyond the solar system and eventually perhaps the galaxy itself.

Our capacity for amazement is all but exhausted. We stifle a yawn when we hear people say that technology has transformed the human environment and much of the natural world beyond easy recognition. Or that it allows man, physically weak as a natural being, to swim faster and deeper than a shark, fly higher and farther than an eagle, and race overland at speeds that shame the swiftest cheetah. We know all this, but so what? These are truths that barely excite. We have what could be called "miracle fatigue," as used to prodigies as we are to the air we breathe.

So far this indifference to technology has not slowed technological innovation itself, but we see another consequence emerging that could be symptomatic of something more serious: the disqualification of the human person.

If man in nature was a physically unimpressive being, in a technological world he appears even less significant. Robots can do many things more efficiently than human workers, and though they, too, wear out and need repair or replacement, they are unaffected by emotions and moral choices.

These comparisons of man and machine are part of a modern mindset that considers all forms of matter—human, animal, and material—to be reducible to the same physical reality. If one accepts this premise, then people simply live and die and there the human story ends without possibility of replay or sequel. By this reasoning, it is as illogical to claim human survival beyond death as it would be to argue that robots have souls.

But anomalies appear when we begin to consider what it means to be a person. We cannot say that persons simply "are," as is the case of material things. Instead, personal reality "happens" sequentially in a biographical and dramatic sense. Persons consist not of fixed being but of the possibilities of being and becoming. Human reality is enmeshed in imagination. Everything truly human must be dreamed before it can be done. Unlike things, people have options; they can decide, they must decide; they can err, repent, love, and create. None of this is possible with things. This means that personal reality is radically superior to the reality of things. But since we humans have always been involved with things and had our greatest successes with them, it is natural for us to try to understand human reality in the same way we have successfully interpreted things. It hasn't worked. We know a lot about things, even things about ourselves, but are still amazingly "illiterate" about our reality as persons.

Article 98: Turning a Deaf Ear or a Blind Eye?

The first rule of life is to be open and alert to reality, especially to other people. We spend much of our time keeping up with what they do and say and, equally important, what they don't do and say. Not to pay attention to what is going on can be not only a selfish unwillingness to share life but also a dangerous mistake. The old saying that what you don't know won't hurt you is a consummate stupidity. The train you don't see approaching the rail crossing or the poison label on the bottle you don't read can do more than hurt you. They can kill you.

But to many things it is better to turn a deaf ear, provided we have first turned an alert ear long enough to know what is going on. If we trust our intuitions, they will quickly distinguish between the true voices that we can count on and the false echoes that lead us astray. No telling how many of life's tragedies occur because we overrule what our heart is telling us.

The world is full of people who go through life trying to recruit us for their pet projects, some a waste, others worthy, but all a mistake if our heart is not in them. And these intrepid souls take a polite hearing for an eventual "yes" and press on all the harder. How easy it is to sabotage our destiny by settling for good things that are not our calling. It is not to our advantage to mask cowardice with courtesy. The courage to respond with a firm and therapeutic "no" up front can save us from a lot of misery later.

The "deaf ear syndrome" is usually the best response to gossips and liars. And we intuitively know who they are. Nothing I know of is more deflating or accusatory to these mongers than the sound of silence. It speaks more eloquently than words.

It takes a steady nerve not to lash back when people attack us publicly. But often an angry reaction on our part is precisely what opponents want, for it opens the way to more accusations and public notoriety and in the end offends everybody and settles nothing. If there is any advantage in the short attention spans of our day, it is that people soon forget the controversy unless we keep fanning the flames.

But turning a deaf ear in the ways I have described it is not the same thing as turning a blind eye to what is going on. Some matters are so morally or legally egregious that as honest people we cannot ignore them. We all know that not to come forth and speak the truth when circumstances demand it is to be an accomplice to wrongdoing. It is not easy, especially in our day when we can flip on the TV and retreat to a world of our choosing. Most of us live in soft comfort, which is always the enemy of hard truth.

Article 99:
Questions about Sports

Maybe you can answer some question that have puzzled me for a long time. Why is it that nearly all modern sports originated in the English-speaking countries? Think of the list: tennis, golf, soccer, cricket, polo, and rugby, all of which either originated or were perfected in Great Britain. And on the other side of the Atlantic, Americans continued the trend by inventing baseball, basketball, and American/Canadian football. If my math is correct, Great Britain and the United States invented or perfected over ninety-five percent of all sports played today. There are others. Jai alai comes from the Basque region of Spain, bowling was already around in ancient Egypt, boxing and wrestling were part of the original Olympic Games in Greece, and lacrosse is, I believe, a legacy of Native

But why the disproportionate contributions of the Anglo world? Perhaps you will suggest that the percentages reflect the imperialistic presence of the British and Americans. But let me point out beforehand that other countries also had empires: Spain, France, Rome, Russia, China, Mongolia, Middle Eastern Caliphates, Ottoman Turks, and others. Yet as far as I know, none of them made substantial contributions to our sports heritage, which hardly existed before the eighteenth century and mostly arose in the nineteenth and twentieth centuries. When soccer first appeared in Spain around 1900, Spanish intellectuals opposed it as a corrupting foreign influence. But it spread anyway, conquering countries far more easily than armies. Today soccer is the most popular sport in practically any country you can name. Not that soccer unites and pacifies nations. The bitterest enemies share the same passion for it. In fact, I recall that it almost caused a war years ago between two Central American countries.

Some have suggested that sports are a substitute for war and that they decline noticeably when real war occurs. But this proposed analog raises as many questions as it answers. For if true, are we then to infer that the Americans and British are subliminally far more warlike than other cultures? But if not, then what took the place of sports in other cultures and in former times? We are back to the same enigma: why are sports an overwhelmingly predominant feature of modern Anglo-American culture?

The fury and enthusiasm of sports may overshadow the rules of the game. We know that sports cannot simply be uncontrolled violence. Without rules there can be no sports. If hunting is a sport, it cannot be indiscriminate slaughter. In this context golf appears to be the strangest sport of all, a different order of competition in which the primary opponent is oneself. All this culminates in a final question, what is the difference between play, a characteristic of nearly all young animals, and sports, which a few humans play and many more watch? I do not have answers. Perhaps you do. If so, would you tell me?

Article 100: The End of Poverty, Hunger, and Disease?

I read recently that the World Bank and its affiliates have announced the goal of ending poverty by 2030. It can be done, they tell us, with a fair system of wealth distribution. The plan calls on each nation to pony up its fair share and asks citizens to back the effort by signing petitions urging governmental compliance. The Stop Hunger Now organization has a similar plan for ending hunger. It is based on the premise that the world already produces enough food to feed everybody. The missing component is an effective system of food distribution. There are similar hopes for the eradication of diseases, some of which—smallpox and polio—have virtually disappeared already.

As I ponder these optimistic possibilities, it occurs to me that our views of these sufferings have changed drastically in recent decades. As children, many of us were told that "starving children overseas would be glad to have those vegetables on your plate." I would have gladly donated mine if there had been a way. There was none and, under pressure, I had to eat them myself. The whole point was to shame American kids into eating their plentiful food, in no way to eradicate world hunger. In that era there was abundant sympathy for impoverished, hungry people, but no one conceived of eliminating hunger, disease, and poverty altogether. After all, they had been around as long as mankind had lived on earth, not as solvable problems but as enduring facts of the human condition itself.

Can these sufferings now be eliminated? That extraordinary possibility has altered our outlook on life. Instead of viewing them as permanent features of human fate, we are beginning to see them as remediable, as wrongs that must be righted. And there is a darker side to this reasoning. If these conditions are wrongs, then there must be someone or something that is causing or exacerbating the wrongs and, therefore, can be blamed and perhaps punished. These conditions have always resonated morally and religiously; now they are also assuming political overtones and hostilities.

As for fatal diseases, we are beginning to think of them not as the natural end, as in olden days, but as accidental, undeserved interruptions of life. Death is becoming a matter of living too soon for cures just out of reach today. And geneticists now tantalize us with predictions of infinitely extended existence, an earthly version of everlasting life. Can we imagine the social and theological upheavals if these predictions become realities?

All these aims are laudable and perhaps possible, but are they realistic? Probably not at this time. The timetable seems hopelessly short. Fair distribution systems of food and resources require an improbable combination of power and goodwill. For power is nearly always subversive of idealism; regimes capable of carrying out massive humanitarian efforts are also capable of suppressing them. It will take, I think, better strategies than the utopian schemes I have seen. Still, we must try; otherwise we become passive accomplices to the ills of this world.

Article 101:
The Insider doctrine

Sociologist Robert Merton describes "The Insider Doctrine" as the belief that only insiders have the right to speak for their group. Only women can speak for women; only members of minorities can represent minorities. "Outsiders" are told to keep their distance and their silence.

The argument wobbles under its own weight. Taken to a logical extreme, we would have to ask ourselves whether we have the right to talk about, say, ancient Greeks, Egyptians, or Romans, or for that matter, anything beyond our immediate experience. The reasoning behind the "Insider Doctrine" is an age-old logical fallacy. Centuries ago philosophers called a solipsism, and it was as invalid then as it is today.

The more valid logic we call common sense tells us that not only do we have the right but also the obligation to concern ourselves with things that matter to us regardless of their origin. And human things—and many things that are not—matter greatly, permanently, and universally.

The "Insider doctrine" became a familiar pattern as one minority after another adopted it. But there were obvious differences when it came to women. To begin with something obvious, women were never a minority, but approximately half the population inseparable in countless ways from the other half.

To apply the "insider doctrine" to women introduced a false, adversarial note into the feminist cause from the beginning. But the success it enjoyed in the cause of true minorities was too tempting to pass up.

The feminist movement was "imitative" in yet another

sense. Instead of elevating politics, business, and public life with feminine grace, elegance, and morality, women equated the masculine vices with freedom and rushed to adopt them. As a result, a coarsening of both sexes is reflected in a general degradation of manners, dress, language, and entertainment.

It is worth pointing out in this context that the American frontier was civilized not by fast-draw gunmen, as Hollywood used to pretend, but by the arrival of women who demanded accountability from men and shifted life from saloons to schools and churches.

In those days women could not vote, but this does not mean they lacked influence. One of paradoxes of history is that women have wielded the greatest influence when they acted privately on those who governed publicly. In more recent times, as women intervene publicly in politics, they tend to do so in imitation of men. Hence the harsh, unfeminine image of many female politicians.

As we see in our circle of family and friends more and more women used, manhandled, addicted, diseased, divorced, abandoned, legally unprotected and financially desperate, we have to ask, is this the freedom women sought? Is their loveless, chaotic, lonely existence really a better life than their grandmothers knew? And are the men who abuse, deceive, and leave them better men than their forefathers? Much has been written about the crisis of women, very little about the decline of manhood. The problems of each sex belong to all and rightfully must be treated by all.

A more pervasive problem, about which much corrective thinking is needed but which I have yet to see acknowledged, is the modern American tendency to funnel human and social problems almost exclusively into political channels. Politics is real, but it is a secondary reality that has a way of offering false solutions to real problems.

Article 102: The Future of Books

Recently I came across a volume of the *Encylopaedia Britannica* in the ashes of riverside campfire. The covers were intact but the pages were wet from rain. My first impulse was to take it with me but then remembered with mixed feelings that I had more books than I could shelve. And what good is an isolated volume today when one can google nearly all the information it contains? For over two centuries beginning in 1768 the *Encylopaedia Britannica* was the gold standard for reliable information. There was something sadly symbolic in the abandoned volume. It was the end of an era. Perhaps I should have given it a proper burial.

It brings up the future of books in general. And the primary question is whether they even have a future. More books than ever are published but fewer read. By the last estimate I saw, over 5,000 books are published yearly in the United States alone. Many of these are self-published, or published on demand, which limits their distribution and visibility. But even mainstream books have limited shelf life. They appear, sell, occasionally are read, and disappear in a matter of weeks. As for readership, according to one survey I saw, close to fifty percent of high school graduates never read another book.

As a former editor and small-press book publisher, I learned which books to publish and which to avoid. Unlike most small presses, ours made money, but only because we followed realistic policies. The failure rate for startup presses approaches ninety percent by the last count I saw.

In an industry where vanity abounds and unrealistic dreams

soar, so do scams. Many companies will take your money and print your book; hardly any can sell it. The usual format for producing successful books consists of two simple steps: (1) begin with a famous person--actor, athlete, politician, or preacher--and (2) shell out money to promote the work. This may include ghost writer fees if the great personality is not a writer. Normally all this must be done quickly. The public has a short attention span, so turnaround and timing are crucial. I could tell war stories of people who approached us too late. Most books of this type are throwaways that cost too much, offer too little, and lack lasting value.

From a broader perspective, it seems to me that the future of books will not be as references like the old *Encylopaedia Britannica*. The electronic media are better than books for that purpose. Instead, it will consist of books that invite one to visit and linger, enjoying the friendship of people who never were or whom we never met. Unlike the throwaways that are here today and gone tomorrow, these books have staying power, growing with us and letting us converse at leisure with the dead and hear their voices with our eyes. Leisure in Greek was *skholé*, our word for school, the school of life.

Article 103: The End of Infinity?

Once upon a time the earth seemed infinite and infinitely mysterious. The classical Greeks believed that beyond the habitable world there stretched an encircling ocean-sea of immeasurable dimensions. With his usual intrepidness Alexander the Great meant to reach its shore. His forces smashed the Persian Empire and several armies in their three-thousand-mile march across Asia. But when they reached India his generals balked. Enough was enough they said. The world was limitless, but they were not. Reluctantly, Alexander turned back, soon died, and his quest passed into history.

Although experienced sailors and learned scholars always knew better, the notion that anything existed beyond the outer ocean was considered heretical until the great age of discovery and exploration. The writings of Clement, Pope from 88 to 99 AD, were excluded from the canonical biblical scriptures partly because he speaks of lands beyond the ocean.

The modern age began with the incorporation of whole new continents and cultures—the Americas, Australia, sub-Saharan Africa, countless islands—into the world's imperial and economic structure. The known world grew immensely larger in several dimensions. Men could reasonably strive for conquests of territory, science, art, and philosophy. The world appeared to be conveniently divided into civilization and savagery, overlords and underlings. If the classical world was defined by infinite mystery, the modern world was a panorama of boundless possibilities for the able and ambitious. It was an optimistic age of conquest and colonization with almost limitless opportunities. Thomas Jefferson looked out on the seemingly endless west of the young United States and declared that centuries must pass before it was full.

He was right in his vision but wrong in his timing. Lands were claimed ahead of schedule. A time came when there were no new worlds to conquer. Every habitable territory became a country, often more fiction than fact, but with its own map coloring and assigned seat in the United Nations. Americans rushed westward until the west ran out. They loved the wilderness, deeply woven into their folklore, but what they loved most they soon destroyed, burying it under asphalt and concrete and imprisoning it within fences. Forests and jungles, once menacing and perilous, were slashed across the world, leaving only shrunken remnants dependent for survival on the protection of nature's old human adversaries.

Perhaps above all others, the American psyche is still fixated on infinity. We long for virginal frontiers and limitless horizons. Shall we find them here on earth or on other worlds? Decades ago we thrilled briefly to men on the Moon, but dead worlds do not long excite restless men and women. Perhaps we shall delight again in new conquests of daring and spirit as yet undreamed of. It is possible, but less likely, that we shall rid ourselves altogether of such boundless urges, learn to live at peace in our finite world, and as Voltaire writes at the conclusion of *Candide*, be content "to cultivate our garden."

Article 104: Unreal Man

Speculation about human reality is at least as old as history. Both biblical writers and Greek philosophers asked, what is man? Neither group got a flattering answer to their inquiries. God's response was a chilling putdown: man is dust and to dust he will return. Plato offered Socrates' cautious definition: "Man is a featherless biped." Whereupon cynical old Diogenes, who mocked the respectable Greek thinkers of his day, plucked a chicken and tossed it in their midst. "There, Plato, is your man."

In the sixth century Boethius described a person as "an individual substance of a rational nature." He was martyred for his Christian faith and is counted among the Saints. But Jesus and the Gospel writers said very little about rationality, emphasizing instead other qualities such as mercy, compassion, forgiveness, and charity.

In different versions, however, Boethius' description has remained definitive over the ages. In the seventeenth century French thinker Rene Descartes made rational human thought—I think therefore I am—the foundation of his philosophy. Today, thanks in part to Boethius, the scientific description of man is *Homo sapiens* ("wise or knowing man"). For most people, intelligence, or IQ, remains—perhaps incorrectly so—the most prestigious human characteristic.

There was more to come. With the triumph of science in modern times another idea blended with classical rationalism: the belief that natural laws governed not only the physical universe but human actions as well. Karl Marx argued that human economic behavior was as predictable and inalterable as the planets in their orbits.

With Darwin, the last trace of human uniqueness seemingly disappeared. Not only was man subject to the same physical laws as other realities, he was himself an animal species, more akin to apes than angels.

Only one thing was wrong with this paradigm: humans did not behave like obedient planets and only occasionally like simians. Someone has said that Karl Marx was the first to disobey Marxist theory. In fact, man essentially lacks the instincts that guide animal behavior, and to the degree that he tries to return to nature and live like an animal, he becomes neither human nor animal but a mere travesty of himself.

This means that everything human must be learned, and thus may be forgotten. A tiger is essentially the same tiger that lived a thousand years ago. But man can always change, can always be more—or less—than he is. And not only in a span of centuries but within his lifetime. He possesses the mysterious capacity to repent, to change his ways, and not only in his faith but in other behaviors as well.

The misunderstanding of human reality begins with the question, what is man? It is the wrong question and leads to the wrong answer. The question is not "what" man is—dust, flesh, physical being— but "who" man is, the person he must decide to be or not to be. For this reason, in order to understand anything human we must tell a story. We are novelists of ourselves and the tale is not complete until the last mortal chapter is written. And perhaps not even then. Unlike any other being we know of, man is always coming into being by means of memory, foresight, and imagination. This means that his reality is also partially unreal. It is a category of reality that has always eluded the laws that govern material things.

Article 105: Aaron Burr, Villain or Victim?

History, it seems, rendered its verdict long ago. Probably Aaron Burr will always be remembered as the villain who killed Alexander Hamilton in a duel. Hamilton's face is on every ten-dollar bill; pictures of Burr are hard to find. But as historian H.W. Brands suggests in his excellent book, *The Heartbreak of Aaron Burr*, that after more than two centuries it may be time to review the extenuating circumstances of the tragedy. The matter is old but also timely, given today's political climate. Their rivalry grew out of the intense hostilities that were emerging in new American Republic. Hamilton belonged to the Federalist Party; Burr favored the Republican-Democratic faction led by Thomas Jefferson and James Madison. The framers of the Constitution had not foreseen the rise of political parties and did not like them. George Washington belonged to neither party and though apparently inclined to Federalist sentiments, disliked both.

Both Burr and Hamilton were Revolutionary War heroes and architects of American independence. Later they were acknowledged as the most prominent attorneys in New York, and according to Erastus Root, arguably the most brilliant men in the nation. Burr tied Jefferson in presidential electoral votes in 1800. Jefferson was declared President, Burr then became the Vice-President. Hamilton continued to scheme against his arch rival whom he saw as the main obstacle in his pathway to national prominence.

There is no doubt that Hamilton provoked the duel by his unrelenting attacks on Burr's character. At first and for as long as gentlemanly forbearance permitted, Burr ignored his rival's vicious comments. But finally Hamilton's public statements became so extreme that to remain silent not only would have cast doubt on Burr's courage but also made him a passive accomplice to the slander. Burr requested satisfaction but left the way open for an honorable reconciliation. Hamilton would retract nothing.

Dueling was illegal in both New York and New Jersey, but because the law was less strictly enforced in the latter state, there, in Weehawken, the antagonists met in July of 1804. Burr was the better shot and Hamilton fell mortally wounded. But both men lost: Hamilton, his life, and Burr his reputation and future.

Jefferson was determined to crush Burr. In 1807 he was tried for treason in Richmond, accused of attempting to create an empire in the West. The case seemed strong, but Justice John Marshall saw to it that the law was applied fairly. Burr was found not guilty.

His troubles continued. His only family, brilliant daughter Theodosia and her son, both died early, depriving him of his only consolation. Unable to rebuild his law practice, he acquired crushing debts and at times went hungry.

In many ways Burr was a man ahead of his time. He believed fervently in the education and advancement of women, and what he foresaw for the West, Andrew Jackson and others achieved decades later. They are heroes; Burr is still a villain. Has history unfairly victimized him?

Article 106:
The Origin of Beauty

Russian novelist Fyodor Dostoyevsky wrote that "The world will be saved by beauty," which leads us to ask two rhetorical questions: first, does this mean that the world is lost and, second, is ugliness to blame for its condition? Rhetorical questions require no answer, but what we can see for ourselves is that in their multiple forms—artistic, personal, and moral—beauty and ugliness contend for cultural supremacy. Today the general consensus among humanistic thinkers is that a "cult of ugliness" prevails.

This does not mean that beauty and ugliness are co-equals. The assumption—and hence the ready insistence—that every controversy has two valid sides is a peculiarly American trait which urges us to tolerate the intolerable in the name of fairmindedness. The relationship of beauty and ugliness is similar to that of heat and cold, light and darkness, substance and shadow. In each case, the first is real, the second, only apparent.

To the many ways that humans differ absolutely or in degree from other species—art, music, language, rationality, clothing—probably we should add humanity's unique sensitivity to visual beauty. Unlike animals, which mate only in seasonal estrus and rut, people desire, in season and out, to "procreate in beauty," as Aristotle wrote.

An abiding question is where and how did human susceptibility to beauty originate? Naturally no one knows for sure, but it seems reasonable to suppose that it resulted, as did speech, from our earliest infantile surroundings. Since our first relationship is usually with our mother or another female caretaker, it stands to reason that the female person was the primary model of beauty. Men were usually more distant and secondary. And this aesthetic hierarchy continues today in linguistic shadings. Women are beautiful; men, only handsome.

Theology offers another argument for the personal origins of beauty. If mankind was the Creator's masterpiece, then it is logical to suppose that the first perfect human persons embodied the aesthetic categories of form, proportion, and harmony. Later these qualities would be abstracted, transmuted, and applied to other beings and inanimate things. To support this line of reasoning we call as witnesses poets who have always sensed that beauty derives from the divine.

But all I have said is auxiliary to the main point. As Thoreau said: "Everything beautiful impresses us as sufficient to itself." Sufficient yet not limited to its sufficiency, and certainly not limited to any utilitarian exploitation of beauty. There is an unquenchable human yearning for beauty greater than pleasurable prettiness. It is an indefinable longing for boundless beauty that transcends common life. But if beauty is an end, it is also a means. As Pope John Paul II put it, "Beauty is a key to the mystery and an invitation to transcendence. It is a call to relish life and to dream of the future." Following this reasoning to its logical conclusion, can we not say that our enthusiasm for beauty is an affirmation of life?

Article 107: Horizons

The horizon separates the real world from the possible, the ideal from the actual. Like the future, which continues as future only as long as it does not enter the here and now, so also the horizon exists only by being as far away from us as possible. Both belong to an odd category of ideal things that exist only by keeping their distance from us. The horizon can be either a limit or an allurement. For some, it entices as tantalizing mystery; for others it marks the outermost boundary of security. In large measure, human life reflects the tension between those content to live in the known reality on this side of the horizontal divide and others eager to pursue the challenges and charms beyond it.

The Nile River was like an umbilical cord to the ancient Egyptians that limited their horizons and blunted their curiosity about the world beyond it. On the other hand, Rome pushed their horizons ever outward until their conquering zeal weakened and they built walls and fortifications to keep out the barbarians. By then the empire had become too vast to expand and too vulnerable to defend. Rome stopped and stagnated as its genius for dominance faltered, trailing broken ideals like flotsam from a sinking ship. Like all civilizations in decline, it was ugly. On the other hand, Egypt, like classical China, had a will for unchanging permanence.

New horizons eventually appear to have a transformative effect on transplanted human psyches, which leads to new styles of life and people. Early observers saw the phenomenon in North America as English settlers morphed into Americans, and others commented on a similar process as Spaniards became Argentineans. One of the great historical transformations, to which history has paid scant attention, began with the returning Crusaders in the thirteenth century. Dazzled by exotic Oriental cultures, they brought back innovations in art, ideas, and agriculture that launched the first European Renaissance. As historian Barbara Tuchman argues persuasively in her book "A Distant Mirror," had it not been for the calamitous Black Death, what we call the Renaissance would have begun with even greater impetus two centuries earlier.

On a personal level, the seashore places in purest relief the horizontal divisions of world. The neat horizontal confluence of sky and sea invites us to inventory and adjust our life with similar simplicity. There we shed our spiritual burdens, as we shed excess clothing, and pledge fresh beginnings. Seashore simplicity allows us to be the children we still are and the philosophers we always were. There are no real contradictions in the duality, for both childhood and philosophy are age-conditioned patterns of curiosity, construction, and delight.

All this means that we are never the solitary beings the old Romantics and Existentialists would have us believe. Instead we shape our life in a creative complicity with the world marked by our horizons. To paraphrase a prominent philosopher, I am I and my horizons.

Authors Bio

Novelist and short story writer, linguist, philosopher, and professor, Harold C. Raley holds degrees (BA, MA, PhD) in English, Foreign Languages, Humanities, and Philosophy. Named Distinguished Professor, he has taught languages, literature, and philosophy in American and foreign universities. His publications include fourteen books of fiction, history, language, and philosophy, and approximately 150 articles and essays on wide-ranging topics in professional journals and newspapers.

Title: Louisiana Rogue
- Author: Harold Raley
- Publisher: Lamar University Press
- Paper Back: ISBN: 9780985255275
- eBook: Kindle
- Pages 306
- Publication Date: April 2013

This wonderfully entertaining picaresque novel by Harold Raley falls in the tradition of rogue literature established by Tom Jones and other early novels. Set in the nineteenth century, Louisiana Rogue will take you on a wild, fast-paced romp through all levels of Cajun society in the 1830s. The title page says the book promises to tell "The Life and Times of Pierre Prospère-Tourmoulin, Picket-pocket, Thief, Gambler, Fugitive, Undertaker, Barber, Doctor, Priest, Prisoner, Bandit, and Count; Latterly penned in his hand for the gentle reader of leisure, Spanning the years 1831-1839" and claims to be translated by Peter Tourmoulin.

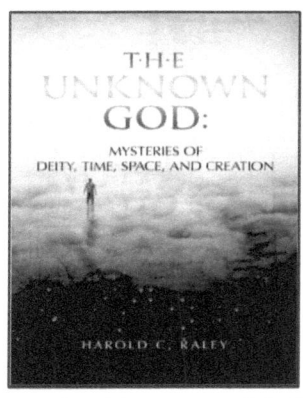

Title: The Unknown God: Mysteries of Deity, Time, Space, and Creation
- Author: Harold Raley
- Publisher: CreateSpace
- Paper Back: ISBN: 9781466273184
- Pages 142
- Publication Date: October, 2011

In his powerful Introduction to The Unknown God, religious thinker and writer Harold Raley makes this unusual request of the reader: "Suspend, if you will, everything you know about God. Put aside for the duration of this reading your traditional theologies and hear a new and more reverent way of thinking about God. When you return to your old understandings, they will have deeper meanings, unless those you once professed were meaningless to start with. If you are unwilling or unable to do as I ask, read no further. This message is not for you. The truth it contains will find you later when it is ready for you and you have been made ready for it." To approach Deity from this radically new perspective--arguably the greatest advance in theological thought of modern times--is to expose and shed light on the baffling paradoxes, improbable notions, and misleading errors not only about God but also about time, space, creation, and immortality. In each of these categories this book offers stunning new insights that incorporate not only the efforts of classical theologians but also the latest discoveries in science. Outline in these advanced insights is a new understanding of human life. By the law of corresponding identities, Raley explains, a more elevated theory of God necessarily means a more elevated theory of mankind. Each of the many themes and aperçus packed into this slender volume could have been a hefty tome. With pristine eloquence Raley reduces them to the essentials, believing as he does that clarity of style is courtesy to the reader.

Title: The Light of Eden:
A Christian Worldview
- Author: Harold Raley
- Publisher: John M. Hardy Publishing Co
- Paper Back: ISBN: 9780979839122
- Pages 196
- Publication Date: May 2008

An inspiring vision of richer Christian life and thought. In the tradition of C. S. Lewis and G. K. Chesterton, this extraordinary book is both a spiritual adventure and an intellectual feast. Packed with illuminating insights and written in beautiful language, The Light of Eden introduces its readers to a vast treasury of creative ideas, innovative concepts, and possibilities contained in Christianity.

Title: The Spirit of Spain
- Author: Harold Raley
- Publisher: Halcyon Pr Ltd
- Paper Back: ISBN: 9780970605498
- Pages 212
- Publication Date: October, 2011

The Spirit of Spain brims with aperçus and revelations, many of them controversial, others startling, all engrossing. From Roman Hispania to the most recent Spanish trends, Professor Raley narrates the unique story of Spanish civilization. Examples of his original thinking include a "phenomenology of Spanish history," a new theory of the Spanish Renaissance, new concepts of Spanish patriotism and nationalism, and a reinterpretation of Spanish "Stoicism." As the book unfolds he also takes many sidelong looks into Hispanic America and offers a new explanation of Spain's relationship to Moslem Al-Andalus and modern Europe. The book culminates in a radical analysis of "Quixotic life" and its unsuspected significance for the post-modern age.

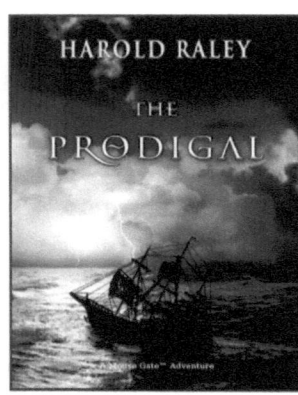

Title: **The Prodigal**
- Author: Harold Raley
- Publisher: Mouse Gate Press
- Paper Back: ISBN: 9781590953402
- eBook ISBN: 9781590953419
- Pages 96
- Publication Date: October, 2016

In the tradition of Crusoe and Sabatini, The Prodigal is a story of the shipwreck and struggle for survival of a young ship's carpenter who escapes one captivity only to fall into more dangerous circumstances. The story unfolds from Boston to Mexico, Cuba, Africa, and back again. At critical points a mysterious stranger intervenes to lend a hand and guide him to his destiny.

Title: Barefoot On A Frosty Morn
- Author: Harold Raley
- Publisher: Mouse Gate Press
- Paper Back: ISBN: 9781590953426
- eBook ISBN: 9781590953433
- Pages 352
- Publication Date: October, 2016

Barefoot on a Frosty Morn is a literary and genealogical tapestry of several families over three centuries. The genealogical threads stretch back to England and France and unfold in step with America's continental expansion. The families crisscross north, south, and west as the tapestry grows in richness and complexity. A final episode sheds light on the earliest roots of the story. The reader has a perspective only partially available to the personalities immersed in the stories. Episodes are woven around some American milestones: the Revolution, the Civil War and WWII. These resonate and enrich but do not hinder the genealogical flow of the novel. In its conception and execution *Barefoot on a Frosty Morn* is unlike any writing before it. It surpasses the limits of history and narrates the essence of the American vision of life.

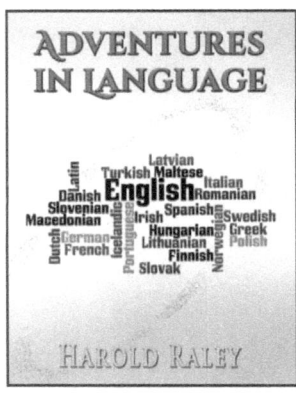

Title: **Adventures in Language**
- Author: Harold Raley
- Publisher: TotalRecall Publications
- Paper Back: ISBN: 9781590955321
- eBook ISBN: 9781590955352
- Pages 216
- Publication Date: October, 2017

In these *Adventures in Language* linguist Harold Raley explores fascinating features of English and many other languages in different cultures and historical eras.

Even though at times I point out obvious errors in the languages as they are currently structured, I realize that the rules of grammar and usage in English or any other living language are, or can be, subject to change. This may not be true of, say, ancient Sanskrit, but then we note that despite its perfection—or perhaps because of it—ancient Sanskrit ceased to be a spoken tongue many centuries ago.

Over the ages thinkers have pondered the qualities that define humanity and set mankind apart from other species. In my view, no stronger case than language can be made for human uniqueness. Animals can communicate and mimic but they cannot speak. Language, sung, recited, or spoken, is archly human, and for that reason also deeply mysterious, beautiful, and fascinating.

Title: **Points Of Light**
- Author: Harold Raley
- Publisher: TotalRecall Publications
- Paper Back: ISBN: 9781590955369
- eBook ISBN: 9781590955376
- Pages 238
- Publication Date: October, 2017

These *Points of Light* centered on the beauty, humor, and mystery of human life present many perspectives flowing out of the unifying philosophical premise that life, not physical reality, is the foundational reality in which all others are rooted.

A noted thinker once said that clarity is the courtesy an author extends to the reader. Insofar as my abilities permit, I have tried to add another kindness: word economy, which I understand to mean saying as much as possible in the fewest words. In those cases in which there is neither clarity nor economy, I alone take the blame.

www.ingramcontent.com/pod-product-compliance
Lightning Source LLC
Chambersburg PA
CBHW030517080526
44586CB00011B/222